Society and Power

STUDIES IN
SOCIOLOGY

Society and Power

by Richard A. Schermerhorn

Western Reserve University

Foreword by

Charles H. Page

Random House

New York

To Barrington Moore, Jr., whose
original reflections on power
have been a stimulus to our generation.

Fourth Printing, February 1964

Library of Congress Catalog Card Number: 61-8786

Manufactured in the United States of America

Editor's Foreword

Sociology is concerned with patterned social relationships, with groups and institutions, with the determinate conditions and consequences of social action. Thus the "field" of the sociologist, in principle at least, stretches across the changing human scene: his guiding concerns reveal themselves, for example, in family life and play, in office and factory, in formal and informal organizations, in the economy and in the polity, in the local community and the larger nation. Within—and between—these several realms the sociologist investigates such pervasive processes as conflict and competition and cooperation; he explores the recurring problems of stability, instability, and change; and in these pursuits he analyzes the functions of various modes of social relationships, including those that involve the capacity of some persons to control the conduct of others. This is to say that the sociologist studies—or should study—*power*.

Power relationships, however, rarely have been the *focus* of sociological attention, especially in the United States. Social philosophers and of course political scientists (whose field is often defined as the study of power) have produced an impressive library on the subject. But the contributions of sociologists—with such notable exceptions as Max Weber and Roberto Michels and Robert M. MacIver, all of whom write in the European tradition and hold high qualifications in disciplines other than sociology—have been sporadic or peripheral. Close examination of fugitive sociological and anthropological discussions of the role of power in social life, together with judicious use of selected works in adjacent fields, undergirds Professor Schermerhorn's successful effort to bring a considerable degree of order to the *sociological* study of power.

Proceeding from a novel analysis of the nature of power and influence, and of the role of both in social control, Professor Schermerhorn brings out clearly, and with apt illustrations, the ways in which power is organized and used in different types of societies, under different sets of circumstances, and by different kinds of social groups. He delineates variations in patterns of power and authority and depicts graphically the dimensions of power, as revealed in the use of naked force on the one hand and cloaked authority on the other. Particularly important today, these matters are discussed with explicit reference to processes and problems of social change. As the Study stresses, power arrangements, legitimate as well as unauthorized, are of strategic significance in a rapidly changing social order.

"Power" is a subject of enormous scope, a fact that increases its susceptibility to easy generalization and impressionistic interpretation. Like "love," power is open territory for all: moralist or analyst, poet or scientist. No work can grasp the whole of it, even within the perspective of a single discipline. And this Study, as Professor Schermerhorn carefully notes, is a *limited* treatment of power and society. But it is, I believe, a highly suggestive sociological introduction to a subject that merits—indeed demands—the close attention of all students.

Charles H. Page

Contents

Introduction

The purpose of this brief study is to provide the groundwork for exploring, from a sociological point of view, the power realities of society, an area that has traditionally been the domain of the political scientist.

Interpretation of the role of power in human affairs has broadened over the years; as early as the nineteenth century, Karl Marx's analysis of economic forces caused even those who disagreed with him to reevaluate the social bases of power and to consider the possibility that political configurations are dependent on deeper-lying societal processes. Later, Max Weber's typological classification of power into traditional, legal, and charismatic forms, illustrated profusely with historical examples, stimulated sociologists, historians, and political scientists to take a more panoramic view of the subject and to extend Weber's analysis into areas formerly neglected by political science. Bertrand Russell's suggestive, though incomplete, review of power realities soon made it clear that these could no longer be treated by any one specialty but were the province of all the social sciences and of philosophy as well. H. D. Lasswell and Abraham Kaplan attempted to codify and unify power theory more systematically but their efforts to keep the study within the usual framework of political science were only partly successful.

The attentive reader observes this approach continually going afield to draw on anthropology, sociology, and economics. Later, from the sociological ranks came Floyd Hunter to portray the power structure of an urban community; repercussions of his research in political science have served to transform many specialists in that field into what appear to be urban sociologists.

Once it is clear that the subject of power is no longer restricted to any one social science, the sociologist becomes aware of how much he has neglected this social dimension of power in his teaching. Introductory texts almost uniformly exclude it (with the possible exception of Blaine Mercer's *Study of Society* and Kimball Young and Raymond Mack's *Sociology and Social Life*). Students in advanced courses must be referred to scattered and heterogeneous sources to acquaint themselves with the fundamental concepts of power. For this reason a short, elementary introduction, such as the one offered here, may prove of real value to the instructor who either lacks the library facilities for acquainting students with necessary materials or prefers to begin with a simpler treatise, sociologically oriented, before sending his students to primary authorities.

The author has deliberately restricted the scope of this

volume to problems of the middle range, excluding the study of power in small group analysis as too strongly oriented to artificial laboratory conditions and the study of international relations as too broad in scope. These limitations must not be interpreted as failure to recognize the importance of either field.

It becomes my pleasant duty to acknowledge intellectual indebtedness to Dr. Barrington Moore, Jr., whose provocative lectures on power find such a poor echo in these pages; also to both Professor Maurice Klain of the Political Science Department and Professor Marvin Becker of the History Department of Western Reserve University for reading parts of the manuscript and giving freely of their suggestions; likewise to Professor James McKee of Michigan State University for his critical and illuminating evaluation of the final chapter.

Finally I extend utmost thanks and appreciation to the editor of the Random House Studies in Sociology, Professor Charles H. Page, whose tireless efforts, critical acumen, and gentle perseverance have been truly Socratic.

R. A. S.

I

The Nature of Power

The sociologist approaches the power dimension in human life, as he does other social phenomena, from a neutral standpoint as far as possible. Briefly, he regards power as neither good nor bad except in the way it is used. By suspending moral judgment from the beginning he can make a more objective analysis.

It hardly needs proof in these days of mass communication (when even a casual reading of the newspaper turns up references to "the power of racketeers," "the power of the courts," "the power of public opinion," "the power of the labor union," "the power of the corporation," and "the power of the Soviet Union") that the notion of power is widespread and frequently talked about. What is less clear is the precise meaning of the idea. Disagreement and confusion are common not only in the interpretation of the phrases quoted above but also in the many scholarly definitions of power.

Power is not a simple notion, though we use the term every day. The purpose of this initial chapter is to reveal the complexities of the familiar term by a little more extended analysis. In beginning with simpler elements and going on to more intricate ones, the aim is to make us aware of the many subtleties involved when we use the term in the well-worn, familiar manner. A little hard thinking at the outset will clarify what power means and furnish us with a workable definition that eventually enables us to use the term with confidence. We can then return to this central definition as a check on our conceptual operations to see if it serves as a point of orientation for what follows.

The Symmetrical Pair Relationship

In our closest and most enduring friendships, the idea of power seldom occurs. Relations between friends are those of easy camaraderie, sharing, mutuality and permissiveness, allowing each member of the pair to be himself, as the phrase goes.

Several things account for this. (1) The relation between friends is one between equals. This means that each person influences (originates action for) the other about as often as the other person influences (originates action for) the first. An even balance in these influences signifies symmetry. (2) Intense liking or affection on both sides supplies the motive for the relation. (3) Both persons refer their behavior to a norm or value standard of cooperativeness and mutuality; they have an ideal of sharing. (4) Rewards predominate over penalties in friends' conduct toward each other. Technically speaking this means that the positive sanctions overshadow the negative.[1]

A departure from any one of these four conditions will probably modify one or more of the others and change the relationship to something slightly different from the accepted pattern of friendship, in the direction of a power relation. Later we shall see why.

A second type of pair relationship also appears to exclude power, but in a different way. Casual relations between two persons may also be symmetrical. Let us say that they appear on the same subway platform and take the same pre-rush-hour train every workday morning, recognizing each other only by sight. Sometimes one enters the train first, sometimes the other; since the crowd is not dense, they do not fight for a place. Each may initiate action for the other almost equally but without involvement. This is the symmetry of indifference.

A third and fourth type of symmetrical pairs, however, reintroduces power, as we ordinarily understand the term. To illustrate the third type, let us take a marriage with the following pattern: husband and wife enchant and repel each other; they "get along neither with nor without each other"; they seem bound together by alternating identifications and antagonisms. Here, though symmetry of influence occurs, it almost certainly involves a power struggle with each manipulating the other and shifting the balance toward negative sanctions from time to time. Similar characteristics often appear in other uncertain pair relations mistakenly called friendships; the

[1] The term "sanction" in sociology conveniently includes both rewards and penalties as reinforcements of desired behavior.

ambivalent marriage is only a dramatic instance of a common type.

The fourth type may be illustrated by two enemies relatively equal in strength, cunning, intelligence, and connections. Their struggle for mastery would therefore show symmetry since they are evenly matched for the initiation of action, yet the object of their efforts would be to destroy each other.

Of the four symmetrical pair relationships, then, two exclude power while the other two include it implicitly or explicitly.

The Asymmetrical Pair Relationship

As might be expected, there are many more asymmetrical than symmetrical pair relations, since symmetry is an ideal limit seldom achieved. The special characteristic of asymmetry is uneven influence, that is, the type of influence in which there is no equality of return effect. Thus one member of a pair initiates more action than the other.

One form of asymmetry in the pair relationship is based on attraction. A single member of the pair, in view of his special qualities attractive to the other, motivates the latter: (1) to want to be with him (popularity), though not necessarily to follow him; (2) to imitate his behavior, using it as a model; or (3) to follow his example or command or both (charisma).[2]

[2] Charismatic leaders are those who have a mysterious "gift of grace" that attracts followers to them almost irresistibly. The term is Max Weber's. Cf. H. H. Gerth and C. Wright Mills, eds., *From Max Weber,* Chapter IX (New York, Oxford University Press, 1946).

There seems to be agreement in common linguistic usage that the first pattern of attraction, popularity, is not identical with power. Research findings support this. Muzafer Sherif found in his two experimental groups of boys in camp that "L" in one group got more sociometric choices than "S" in the same group although the latter "was the acknowledged leader of the group and became the focus of power because of his undisputed authority over L and other high-status members."[3] Thus while L was more popular, S had more power. Popularity as such, then, does not necessarily mean power; it must be supplemented by other qualifications.

The idealized model (example 2) is a marginal case. To the extent that he affects behavior in the direction of a "role model," he seems to have power, though his awareness of this may be nil. If he issues no commands or orders, he is like the popular figure. To the extent that he embodies a norm or ideal already enshrined in the culture in general, or in the other member of the pair in particular, he has greater power than the popular figure and moves toward the charismatic position. It is the instability of the idealized figure that places him on the margin.

The charismatic leader, on the other hand, is unquestionably endowed with authority (socially sanctioned power). He attracts his follower or followers not only because he has so-called personal magnetism but because he embodies, often in novel ways, well-established values. Another feature of the charismatic leader is that his influence, more often than not, extends to a wide circle of individuals and becomes a social force.

[3] Muzafer Sherif and Carolyn W. Sherif, *An Outline of Social Psychology,* rev. ed., p. 197 (New York, Harper & Bros., 1956).

A second form of asymmetry in the pair relationship occurs through pressure or urgency from above and submission or obedience from below. From the standpoint of the one who is influenced, the attitude is remarkably different from attraction. In the case of attraction there is spontaneity, while under pressure or urgency there is effort and constraint. Five sub-forms of this pressure relationship may be listed: (1) submission to a leader or dominant figure who embodies informal group norms; (2) submission to a leader who is an expert, who has rational qualifications; (3) submission to a leader in view of his office, that is, to an institutional figure; (4) submission to a person because of his strength or superior ability to use violence; (5) submission to a dominant figure as a matter of habit.

In the first three cases it is important to notice two key features of the relationship: power flows downward from a superordinate or leader to a subordinate or follower, and it is characterized by authority. Authority, as already noted, has a superindividual quality since it embodies norms or values of an entire group or the society at large. In *Street Corner Society,* which describes the Norton Street gang, William F. Whyte, Jr., has made it quite clear that Doc, the dominant leader, kept his position because he objectified in his own person the group's demands and standards: generosity, fighting ability, skill in bowling, and fairmindedness.[4] Informal though the gang was, it had its accepted norms and rules for what conduct should be, even though they were not as carefully spelled out as they would be in a

[4] William F. Whyte, Jr., *Street Corner Society; The Social Structure of an Italian Slum* (Chicago, University of Chicago Press, 1943).

more formal organization. The second subtype, where an individual submits to a dominant figure because he embodies rational norms, includes such cases as the doctor-patient or lawyer-client relationship. Here the expert has a superordinate position and the less expert one accepts his advice or command when convinced of his special knowledge or skill. Finally, in the third subtype the subordinate submits to the leader because the latter holds a certain office; the boss, the policeman, the president of an organization. Many persons may hold this office or institutional position in rotation (some person must fill it, not necessarily any particular person); whoever occupies the position will have the authority (the power) of that office.

In the relation of pressure or urgency that characterizes the three subtypes just mentioned, the subordinate experiences constraint or respect rather than simple liking or attraction. He feels a certain ambivalence, with at least latent resistance or antagonism. Acceptance of authority requires a definite effort on the part of the one who submits.[5]

The fourth type of asymmetrical pair relationship is straightforwardly coercive. When the gunman pushes a revolver into the ribs of a cashier, he is threatening violence which he quite obviously is prepared to use. If the cashier submits, it is because the conflict is uneven with the greater strength in the hands of the gunman. Here again is the presence of an enemy but this time it is an enemy with a preponderance of force on his side. Submission may be instantaneous but here it is re-

[5] The point is clarified and elaborated in George C. Homans, *The Human Group,* pp. 212-214 (New York, Harcourt, Brace & Co., 1950).

luctant and fearful; it lacks the credence of principle that accompanied the obedience to authority. In the coercive relation the subordinate figure regards the superordinate's power as illegitimate.

Finally there is the fifth type of asymmetrical pair relationship: the casual and habitual, taking place without emotional involvement. As custom and usage make it possible for the subordinate to take orders as a matter of course, he comes to accept such directions as ordinary, everyday adjustments more or less outside the focus of his attention. On the way to the office the clerk follows the instructions of the subway guard, traffic policeman, or elevator starter while planning his next vacation. He continues planning when receiving his batch of work for the day and the instructions that go with it. Half the day may pass before the clerk gives his full attention to what he is doing in the office, yet he has been taking orders from one person after another. Routine often dulls the response to authority and power figures by whittling them down to manageable size and working out conventional reactions to them. In time the submission to one dominant figure after another becomes an unthinking custom; as many of the other asymmetrical relations take on this habitual form, society runs more smoothly and has a more predictable order than it would have if every response to authority were made with the full awareness that accompanies its first impact. Probably it is necessary for this habitual reaction to occur if the basis for regular order in society is to be more than a mere hope.

The discussion thus far is given summary form in Figure 1.

Several important conclusions emerge from analysis

Figure 1

Influence and Power in the Pair Relationship

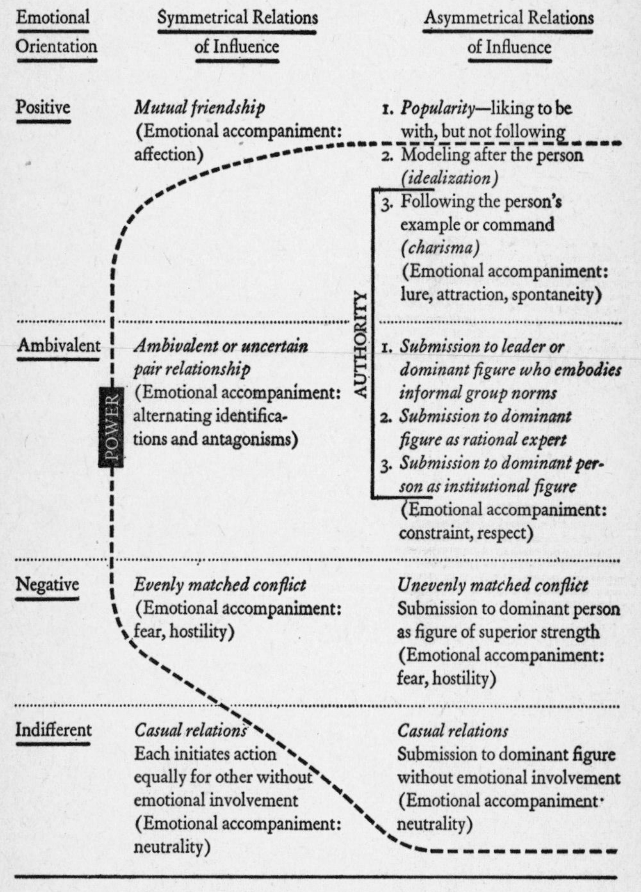

KEY: All relations portrayed are those of influence; those within the broken line are also relations of power. Note the limited set of relations subsumed under authority.

of Figure 1. (1) Power is a type of influence but not identical with it. (2) Power is colored and modified by the scheme of values, norms, or standards accepted by the persons in interaction. Where these values show at least some consensus or agreement, power is then stabilized in the form of authority. (3) Since ambivalent or negative (hostile) reactions are more frequently encountered than positive (affectional) reactions, power usually, though not always, implies some conflict or friction. (4) Exceptions to this conflict occur where power results from attraction to a dominant person, the typical form being charisma. (5) The pair relationship does not occur in isolation; it appears in the context of society.

In any given case, one or both members of the pair represent values or norms of a group, institution, or society transcending them. That is, what each individual does is more than a singular, unique set of acts; it arises from his cultural learning and is therefore the expression of a role. Since he acts as a group member and not purely in his own individual capacity, his behavior is patterned by group expectations, loyalties, preferences, and beliefs. Thus it is impossible to discuss pair interaction by itself; the reader may have noted the references to gangs, occupations, offices, and other wider social contexts. There are even crucial cases where a power clash between two individuals epitomizes a major conflict of social forces, as in the case of David and Goliath, or two diplomats of contending countries, or a labor leader and a corporation executive.

Before moving on to the wider social field, however, it will be useful to summarize our results so far in a diagram that indicates the interrelationship of our variables in a somewhat different way. A second look at the assortment from a different perspective can perhaps clarify a number of interrelationships that were obscure in Figure 1.

Figure 2

The Skewed Curve of Power Relations

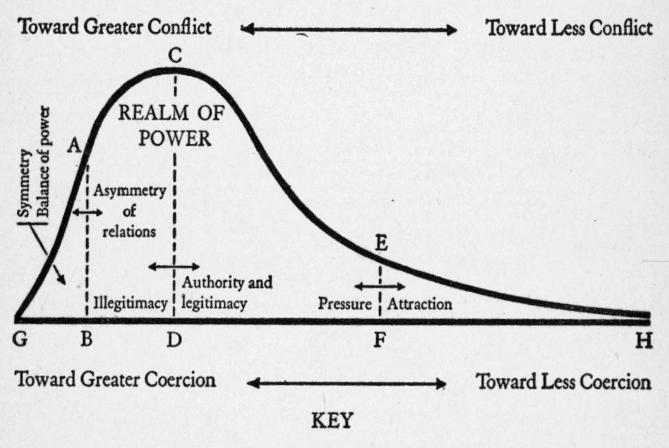

KEY

1. GAB Evenly matched conflict of coercion or violence.
2. GCD Illegitimate power wielding.
3. BACEH Unequal initiation of action. Asymmetry. Domination and submission.
4. DCEH Power tempered or partially stabilized by norms and values. Authority and Legitimacy.
5. GCEF Area of greater or lesser friction and conflict, decreasing toward EF and increasing toward G. Included under "pressure."
6. FEH Power by attraction rather than pressure or friction. Charisma the special example.

A skewed curve differs from the normal bell-shaped curve by having a greater frequency distribution on one side of the hypothetical midpoint than it has on the other. Figure 2 is skewed toward (1) asymmetry (BACEH) and (2) pressure or conflict (GCEF). If this account is reasonable (and it must be provisional, since power theory is incompletely developed), it would follow that these are the two modal characteristics of power. In other words, they are the attributes most frequently found as definite features of power relations.

Since the element of pressure or conflict expresses itself in the predominant use of negative sanctions, we may define power as the processual relation between two parties modally characterized by (1) asymmetrical influence, in which a perceptible probability of decision rests in one of the two parties, even over the resistance of the other party; and (2) the predominance of negative sanctions (threatened or actual) as a feature of behavior in the dominant party.

We then require a supplement to this abstract definition. When interaction departs from the stated mode, it may do so in one of two directions and still retain the quality of power. In the first place, it may vary in the direction of symmetry, in a balance of power. Under this first condition the relationship is still that of power as long as the other modal characteristic is present, that is, as long as negative sanctions prevail. Conversely, interaction can depart from the stated mode in the direction of attraction and away from the variable of negative sanctions, pressure, or conflict. The submissive party in this case is no longer pressured but lured. In this second instance the interaction is still one of power since the other variable, asymmetry, is inherent in the situation. In summary: whatever the deviation from either of the modal characteristics, power relations are still present as long as one of the two variables, asymmetry, or negative sanctions, still remains.

Power and Social Control

In the past, political scientists have analyzed the subject of power more thoroughly than the sociologists have but as the broader implications of the field become more apparent, the necessity arises to relate power to social processes other than those of government. Sociology itself, in the past, has approached the problem in terms of what is called social control. However, the designation social control has certain implications, not always fully stated, that limit its use. In the first place, control is too often interpreted as the use of power and influence to alleviate friction, attain order, or achieve equilibrium in the social process. In the second place, the term connotes dealing with a *fait accompli,* or being concerned with past and present. Power seems to have more relevance to a future dimension; as a concept it has a more dynamic quality, more thrust and activism. Robert Bierstedt speaks of power as always potential.[6] While this view is too extreme, it errs in the right direction, for although power may be regarded as either potential or actual, it is never wholly actual, because its vigor presages future changes. Control, on the other hand, seems to imply an actual or completed process. Sociology would have had quite a different history if it had chosen power instead of control as a major category.

For some years, sociologists have tended to think of society as a configuration or system kept in partial balance either by the reciprocal nature of social interaction (the

[6] Robert Bierstedt, "An Analysis of Social Power," *American Sociological Review* 15:730-738, p. 733 (December, 1950).

model proposed by R. S. Park and E. W. Burgess) or by patterns of maintenance similar to those of an organism (Talcott Parsons' view). In either case the stability is taken as the point of departure and change is explained as the series of internal adjustments or readjustments by which social order is maintained. The study of power, however, reverses the emphasis by assuming that change is the starting point and that order or equilibrium is a by-product of the ceaseless quest for power by individuals, groups, institutions, and nations. If we assume as primary an inherent instability in human affairs, we shift the emphasis to the irregular, dynamic, and asymmetrical aspects of the social process and abandon the preoccupation with equilibrium which seems to impose more order on social interaction than we actually find there.

In this first chapter we have identified the object of our study by a simple analysis of interpersonal relations. The next task is to consider the operation of power in somewhat larger human aggregations, and the way in which it generates new social forms. Anthropological studies of preliterate societies furnish important clues, and in the next chapter some of the anthropologist's discoveries that reveal the working of power in simpler societies will be explored. We can then go on to analyze the role of power in more complex situations.

II

Power Centers or Structures

Returning for a moment to the definition of power given in Chapter I, let us examine the words party and parties. One party can exercise influence over another in a pair relationship, as noted. But now the wider meaning of the term party should be emphasized since it can designate either an individual or a group. (Since some groups operate through institutions, here group is understood to include institutional arrangements as well.)

Four Power Alternatives

Because of this dual meaning of party, we are presented with four logical possibilities: (1) the behavior of an individual may dominate the behavior of another individual; (2) the behavior of an individual may dominate the behavior of a group; (3) the behavior of a group may dominate the behavior of an individual; (4) the behavior of a group may dominate the behavior of another group.

In the first case, if a boy won't eat until his mother turns on the television set, he has power over his mother. In the second case, if several members of a club decide to have a picnic but one person in the organization talks them out of it and into a swimming party instead, that individual has power over the club. In the third case, if the majority of a union votes to raise the annual dues and one of those who voted against the measure nevertheless pays the increased assessment the union has power over that member. In the fourth and final case, if a real-estate lobby puts enough pressure on a state legislature to defeat a bill for higher property taxes, the lobby has power over the legislature.

Some of these dominant influences may be operating simultaneously in a given case; they are often separable only in analysis. It is important to recognize that power may function in all four ways and thus transcend the purely interpersonal field of events. On the other hand, to say, as Robert Bierstedt does, that "the focus of power is in groups" and therefore in intergroup relations alone would eliminate power from interpersonal relations entirely and restrict it to the fourth possibility above.[1] A broader connotation for the term would seem more reasonable.

Bierstedt is more persuasive when he declares that the source of power in human society is threefold: "(1) numbers of people, (2) social organization, and (3) re-

[1] Robert Bierstedt, "An Analysis of Social Power," *American Sociological Review* 15: 730-738, p. 732 (December, 1950).

sources,"[2] particularly where intergroup relations are concerned. In general, a group large in numbers with cohesive organization and adequate means will overcome the opposition of another group deficient in those characteristics. Nevertheless, unless what is meant by "resources" is clear, this concept could well restrict power to the intergroup field alone. Since Bierstedt has not spelled out the meaning of "resources" in detail, we must consider the point more fully.

Review of the evidence leads to the provisional conclusion that there are five types of resources that can be used to advance or to strengthen a power position: (1) military, police, or criminal power with its control over violence; (2) economic power with control over land, labor, wealth, or corporate production; (3) political power with control over legitimate and ultimate decision-making within a specified territory; (4) traditional or ideological power involving control over belief and value systems, religion, education, specialized knowledge, and propaganda; and (5) diversionary power with control over hedonic interests, recreation, and enjoyments.[3] Even brief inspection of these five power resources makes it clear that they are available to individuals as well as to groups; it is equally obvious that all these resources are socially exercised.

Assuming that power is a dynamic process, we may then ask if it tends to repeat itself in easily identified

[2] Ibid, p. 737.

[3] Adapted with revisions and alterations from Bertrand Russell, *Power, A New Social Analysis* (New York, W. W. Norton, 1938) and from lectures of Barrington Moore, Jr., at Harvard University, Spring 1957.

ways. The answer is yes, though the patterns at times overlap. The power process frequently crystallizes into more or less stable configurations designated as centers or structures of power. The rest of this chapter will review some of those patterns in a kind of power-map. Such an overview precedes detailed exploration: a map, of course, is not a true picture of reality but only an outline to be filled in. How, then, does power get shaped, patterned, and organized? Answering this question will provide a broad, general panorama of the power process and furnish the social bearings necessary for further analysis.

Power in the Simpler Societies

Julian Steward, in his account of social evolution, writes that "unifamilial and lineage social forms are succeeded by multifamilial communities, bands, or tribes, and these, in turn, by state patterns." [4] Since there is little but conjecture about the unifamilial groups, it seems better to begin with small, multifamilial communities as the prototype of the simpler societies, especially those with food-gathering, hunting, or fishing as their economic base. Since such societies, being nonpastoral and nonagricultural, have little or no economic surplus, mutuality and sharing become mandatory. It is not too far amiss to say that communal poverty or the democracy of scarcity is characteristic of such simple societies. Let us call them

[4] Julian H. Steward, "Evolution and Process," *Anthropology Today, An Encyclopedic Inventory,* A. L. Kroeber, ed., p. 314 (Chicago, University of Chicago Press, 1953).

participant societies on the premise that most adult members participate in day-to-day decisions.[5]

A brief glance at some of these societies will reveal certain typical forms of interaction. Among the Copper Eskimos, for example, the group of families living together reduces the power of the individual to insignificance. "The Eskimo is intolerant of anything like restraint. Every man in his eyes has the same rights and the same privileges as every other man in the community. One may be a better hunter, or a more skillful dancer, or have greater control over the spiritual world, but this does not make him any more than one member of the group in which all are free and theoretically equal."[6]

Among the Keraki of Papua the local group has a head man who does not issue orders but plays the part of a leader.[7] Certain groups of Eskimos and the southern Bushmen recognize temporary chiefs with authority limited to a specific emergency.[8] In northwest Bushman territory, where local groups are larger, "a hereditary chief is acknowledged. Here, however, the office is most

[5] The term "participant" is preferable to "communal" which too often implies a lack of private property and that is rarely found in any society, even though it has been attributed to early man by a number of Marxist writers. See M. J. Herskovits, *Economic Anthropology, A Study in Comparative Economics,* Chapters XIV, XVI and pp. 500-501 (New York, A. A. Knopf, 1952).

[6] Diamond Jenness, *The Life of the Copper Eskimos,* Report of the Canadian Arctic Expedition, 1913-18, Vol. XII, Part a, pp. 93-94 (Ottawa, F. A. Acland, 1922).

[7] F. E. Williams, *Papuans of the Trans-Fly,* p. 113 (London, 1936).

[8] A. Goldenweiser, *Anthropology, An Introduction to Primitive Culture,* p. 376 (New York, Crofts, 1937) and M. J. Herskovits, *Man and His Works, The Science of Cultural Anthropology,* p. 338 (New York, A. A. Knopf, 1948).

rudimentary, and since 'no tribute or services are rendered to the chief . . . ,' it is apparent that his position brings him no added participation in the total store of goods produced by his group. The reason is simple: the Bushmen produce no surplus. Consequently the chief is 'a leader rather than a ruler,' and it is by force of his personality rather than by his control of tribal resources that he makes effective such authority as he may theoretically possess."[9]

In groups like these social equality has reached a practical maximum, with each member sharing in the activities of the band or community, and with each having close and intimate acquaintance with every other member. There is maximum surveillance of what each member does, close cultural bonds establishing unity through defense against attacks from outside, and cementing of mutual interests through assemblies or ceremonies where food is shared and solidarity celebrated. Such groups furnish a human aggregation with a consciousness of kind in group values and sentiments. Formal organization is probably not even conceived of; disputes between subgroups are settled informally and quickly to prevent a rupture of unity against enemies from without. In this atmosphere of one for all and all for one, tradition and consensus are highly developed and power is diffused throughout the local group as a whole. Separate interests of individuals are kept under control and leaders rise to prominence only under special conditions (usually emergencies) when they help the entire group achieve immediate goals. Richard T. LaPiere has stated the case well: "In all peaceable groups, the persons who exercise

[9] M. J. Herskovits, *Economic Anthropology,* op. cit., p. 399.

leadership through a power structure have usually acquired their powers—which are characteristically indirect and undefinable—by having demonstrated their ability to get the group out of predicaments."[10]

Such contingencies in participant societies usually require persons who can draw on one or more of three resources: economic, religious, or military. The community highly prizes any abilities and skills in these fields and will give temporary or partial grants of power to leaders who can make use of them. A grant of power lasts during the crisis or as long as the leader is successful. In day-to-day relations, however, the participant society distributes power rather evenly throughout its membership, allowing exceptions only when everyone will profit by them. A suitable name for this set of relations is proto-democracy.

Participant societies are thus at one end of a continuous scale ranging from proto-democracy to highly autocratic forms. In summary, participant societies are characterized by:

Reliable consensus
Cooperative values
No separate institutions
Dominance of the social whole over its members
Minimal sanctions
One major, diffuse power field
Predominance of ends over means
The total society as the major in-group
Little or no social stratification

[10] Richard T. LaPiere, *A Theory of Social Control,* p. 178 (New York, McGraw-Hill, 1954).

Societies of Greater Magnitude

With the development of larger, more complex societies, two notable features change the nature of their organization: multiplication of numbers and a shift to a pastoral, agricultural, or mixed economy. The two are mutually supportive. It is impossible to support a greater population unless there is a greater regularity of food supply controllable by man: the possibility of surpluses is introduced. Conversely, a more adequate food supply enables a population to increase beyond the narrow confines of the tiny participant society. Enlargement of the group can take place either by simple population growth or by a conquest that joins together two or more tribes or peoples. The increase in numbers leads to greater difficulty of communication, which weakens the maintenance of consensus. There is less social pressure to equalize and share alike, and at the same time less individual guilt about pressing egoistic advantage.

Changes of this kind permit segmental power centers or structures to appear. In other words, individuals or families with special aptitudes for, or unique access to, the important power resources will put them to greater and greater use, thus building up fields of influence that elevate them above their fellows.

How the process works can be observed most clearly in the cases of three kinds of resources: military, economic, and religious.

If a tribe is surrounded by one or more enemies, it will greatly value the leader who has such talents as deploying men, concocting strategies of ambush and encirclement, or probing the foe's special weaknesses in combat. After a notable victory, such a leader will very likely be honored with special gifts and privileges: tracts of land, additional wives, or herds of cattle. Once these privileges become his, they form the center of an interest[11] and this interest perpetuates itself. To have more land, wives, or cattle than his colleagues eventually becomes a right that he will defend if it is threatened and that he will extend through aggrandizement if he can. One way to do this is to train his sons in the military art to retain the privileges in the family, which then becomes known as a warrior group, separated from lesser families of the community.[12]

Similarly, a skilful herder or tiller of the soil may accumulate larger herds or land resources than his neighbors, and with his greater wealth gain other advantages, more wives, for example. Polygamy increases his labor force with women and children who make it possible to till more fields and care for larger herds. These forms of wealth enable their owner to practice hospitality on a greater scale than before, adding diversionary power to economic power.[13] On the other hand, less fortunate or less successful families can become indebted to those with greater assets; a family having a succession of bad harvests may be forced to borrow from a more affluent family and may even become slaves to pay off the debt. At times, funeral expenses may be so great that persons pawn themselves or family members to assure themselves that the

[11] An interest may be defined as a pattern of demands and expectations arising from a special social position. Such demands and expectations serve to maintain or extend the power of the individual or group occupying that position.

[12] Gunnar Landtman, *The Origin of the Inequality of the Social Classes,* p. 59 (Chicago, University of Chicago Press, 1938).

[13] Ibid, p. 72.

ceremonies are observed. Young men who lack the bride price may become slaves of their future wives' families until the price is paid.[14]

Special knowledge of the supernatural also figures prominently in the accretion of special interests. The user of magic, who can call on unseen forces to cast love spells, cure diseases, bring better crops, or produce military victory, may build up a power center of his own. We are told that the word of the East African priest is "potent for life and death. At his command—or rather suggestion—the village is removed; men, women and children are slain or enslaved; wars are begun and ended."[15]

Such examples show how power structures develop. And they give point to the definition of a power structure as a temporarily stable organization of power resources permitting an effectual directive control over selected aspects of the social process.

Certain dynamic tendencies that seem to be inherent in the growth of power structures are now worth noting:

(1) Power can be easily transformed from one type to another. Control over violence can be converted into power over land; likewise control over wealth can be transmuted into control over diversionary resources; and control over the belief system (in this case, the supernatural) can have decisive influence over wealth or military operations. These transformations introduce important changes in the way the members of the society interact.

(2) Power is cumulative; one type of power tends to adhere to other types, eventually to form a composite

[14] Ibid, Chapter XIII.
[15] Quoted from De Chaillu in Landtman, op. cit., p. 124.

power structure. In other words, holding one sort of power advantage makes it possible (and probable) to acquire other kinds of power advantage. Power in any field tends to spread to other fields in ever-widening circles. The merging of power structures initiates new forms of change in society.

(3) The development of a power structure may give rise to an opposite structure. That is, opposition or resistance to one power structure can become the potential for new power structures. This reaction produces movement and countermovement, sometimes on a small scale, sometimes spreading to the entire society, or even beyond it.

(4) Interests possess a peculiar duality or instability, since they have both public and private aspects. Military prowess, for example, is a source of interest for the group as a whole because it concerns the very survival of the community. The leader whose interests are centered in military prowess may stress its value to the community or its public importance, while it also brings him special advantages or privileges. The stronger the group consensus, the greater the stress on the public aspects of this interest; the weaker or more confused the group loyalties, the greater the stress on its more private or egoistic aspects. This duality of interests allows the development of autocratic power under the guise of social emergencies. Harold D. Lasswell and Abraham Kaplan refer to the two forms as "principled" and "expediency" interests, noting that in social movements, the principled interests are emphasized for outsiders, while expediency interests are stressed within the group striving for power.[16]

[16] H. D. Lasswell and A. Kaplan, *Power and Society, A Framework for Political Inquiry*, pp. 42-43 (New Haven, Yale University Press, 1950).

(5) As collective participation in decisions decreases, the decision-making function is assumed by smaller groups who take over responsibility for the more or less unorganized mass. In other words, there is a trend toward oligarchy. As Gaetano Mosca has said, "In reality the dominion of an organized minority, obeying a single impulse, over the unorganized majority is inevitable. The power of any minority is irresistible as against each single individual in the majority who stands alone before the totality of the organized minority . . . A hundred men acting uniformly in concert, with a common understanding, will triumph over a thousand men who are not in accord and can therefore be dealt with one by one."[17] Segmental power structures tend to cluster about the actions of organized minorities or oligarchies in more complex societies.

These five characteristics indicate the dynamic tendencies of power reactions and how they initiate changes in the social process. Large, complex societies display these trends more distinctly than participant societies because they have the following social patterns:

Indecisive consensus
Value composites or clashes
Developing governmental institutions
Mixed forms of dominance
Increase of sanctions in specific areas
Plurality of unequal, segmental power structures
Growing value disagreement over means and ends
Multiplication of in-groups within the society
Variable social stratification

[17] Gaetano Mosca, *The Ruling Class,* p. 53 (New York, McGraw-Hill, 1939).

Power Structures and Levels of Action

We have observed, in the transition from participant to more complex societies, considerable differentiation of segmental power structures. This can be expressed symbolically in Figure 3.

Figure 3

Power Structures and Levels of Action I

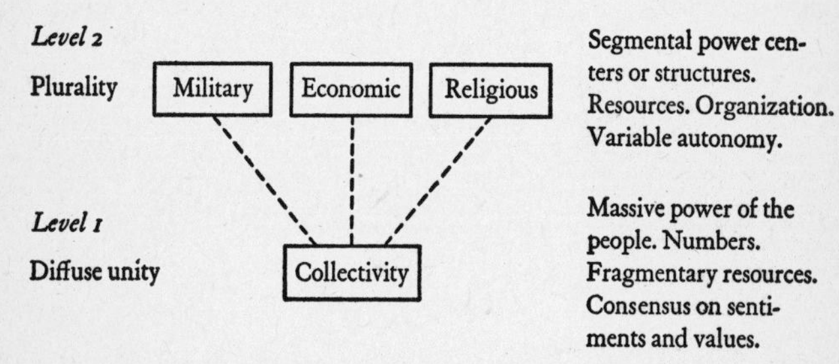

A distinction can now be made between the level of action of the people and of "the powers that be." The collective mass of the community members has the advantage of numbers, some resources, and agreement on the whole body of preferences and selective desires incorporated in the value system. This shapes and determines which of the segmental power centers will have the most appeal or prestige and therefore what types of obedience will be most likely. External circumstances will have a great deal to do with this process: the presence of powerful enemies may tilt the balance toward the military; differences in land resources may lead to a rapid concentration of wealth in a few families so that economic power carries more weight. The energy and resoluteness of leaders in the segmental power structures in advancing their interests are another important factor determining the forms of obedience. As leaders arise, they quite often develop the advantages of greater proportional resources or discipline of organization. By means of such resources they can gradually establish independence and autonomy from the community as a whole; in extreme cases their autonomy enables them to exploit the people at will.

Actual power relations, however, rarely remain at this two-level stage. Both the tensions of interest and the drive for social order push the society toward a three-level organization. Any struggle between the segmental centers of power is likely to continue until either a single one or a coalition achieves victory. Interests remain unsatisfied until they are solidly entrenched or buttressed in what at least appears to be a stable organization of power. In terms of group survival, too, an unrelieved plurality is not satisfactory because it perpetuates a conflict that might tear the society apart. A new level of action may then appear (see Figure 4).

A diagram, lacking movement, cannot show that one of the segmental power structures (sometimes merging two or more) usually becomes the ruling element in the state or governmental institution. The rise to political power of military or economic leaders is more or less self-evident, but religious leaders also gain high authority. Priests who are outstanding for prophecies or miracles attain high position, as for example in the judiciary in Hawaii, Nigeria, and Guinea; among the Indians of the American Northwest coast, they are the warrior chiefs.[18]

[18] Landtman, op. cit., p. 219 and H. H. Turney-High, *Primitive War, Its Practice and Concepts,* p. 110 (Columbia, S. C., University of South Carolina Press, 1949).

Figure 4

Power Structures and Levels of Action II

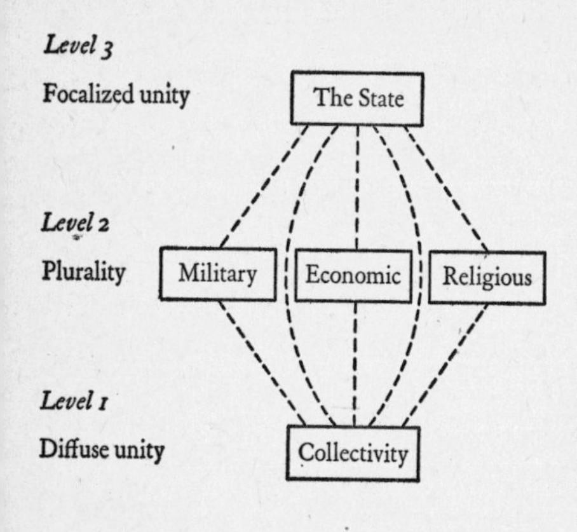

Unified or centralized government. Variable autonomy.

Segmental power centers or structures. Resources. Organization. Variable autonomy.

Massive power of the people. Numbers. Fragmentary resources. Consensus on sentiments and values.

Preeminent leaders in one of the segmental power structures, with an entourage of family members and associates, commonly assume responsibility for "holding the community together, safeguarding its food supply, and guaranteeing peace within and without its borders."[19] Legitimacy is frequently assured to the ruling group by the tacit acquiescence of the people rather than by an explicit grant of power from them. Unless the dominant group was already regarded as having just claims to leadership, it would not be fully certified in the state. Authority is validated first at the two-level stage and becomes more formally recognized when it is concentrated in the state, government, or the political institution. This sort of centralized power may come into existence with or without the conquest of one society by another; in the case of conquest, the problem of legiti-

[19] Julius E. Lips, "Government," *General Anthropology,* Franz Boas, ed., p. 490 (Boston, D. C. Heath, 1938).

macy is more problematical in the early stages.

Every complex social system of the type under discussion contains many currents of conflict in which individuals and groups struggle to consolidate or enlarge their interests. Contention between the different levels generates ceaseless change in the alignments and coalitions of various power centers. The permanence of the structure depends on its context; whether the predominance of power is found at the second or third level depends on the variables already suggested. When the main lines of communication and influence run from level two to three, the governing power tends to be monarchical, aristocratic, or oligarchic; when they proceed from level one to two, it is formal or weak; when they extend from level one to three (as indicated by the curved lines in Figure 4), it is democratic. Of course, a number of combinations or permutations is possible.

An African Example

So far our account of power structures has been schematic, sketching the main lines of development from simpler societies in the early stages of evolution toward more complex and highly articulated types. In order to make the discussion concrete, two African societies corresponding to the two different levels are singled out and I. Schapera's comparison of them is presented in a short summary.[20] This will give more substance to our abstract, morphological, or map-like scheme. In Table A

[20] I. Schapera, *Government and Politics in Tribal Societies* (London, Watts, 1956).

Table A

Tribal Variations in Power Patterns
(Bushmen and Hottentot)

Tribe, Composition, and Economy	Group Dispersion and Population	Power Forms
Bushmen		
Kin societies Hunting and food gathering	Bands of 50-100, each self-governing. Four northwest tribes each with many bands. 8,000 pop. Each band has clearly defined territory of about 200 sq. mi. In dry season, families wander separately; at other times the band moves as a unit.	Chief is head of extended family. "Part-time chief." Most affairs, including warfare with other bands, managed by all adult males. Chief is "executive officer" of the band. Chief has ritual duties. Chief has no legislative or judicial functions. Public life of chief controlled by adult males. No social classes.
Hottentot		
Multiple kin societies with some immigrants and conquered people from other tribes	Tribes of 500-2,500. Nine tribes in 1850. Tribes sometimes together but camp in dispersed groups of 200-300 as much as 20-30 mi. apart. No clear boundaries	Chief is head of a senior clan (clan is *primus inter pares*). Chief has no ritual function. Chief has no control over land tenure. Some chiefs win

Table A (continued)

Tribe, Composition, and Economy	Group Dispersion and Population	Power Forms
Hottentot		
Pastoral (cattle and sheep) supplemented with hunting and collecting	but use-rights to specific water holes and fountains. Eventually settled in tribal centers at the most reliable fountains.	power by usurpation. Hereditary chieftainship not automatic. If there is no kinsman available for chief's position, it goes to a member of the leading family in the clan next in rank. Distinct social classes. Hottentots are "citizens" while resident Bushmen and Bergdama are "servants."

the Bushmen illustrate our category of participant societies, and the Hottentot the more complex social forms.

A glance at the Hottentot pattern reveals an important departure from the formal scheme outlined in the text; instead of segmental power resources, there are kinship groups or clans. These clans are multi-purpose or relatively undifferentiated groups, but they are intermediate power centers nevertheless and constitute a case of level two in the power structure. The fact that the problem of succession to the chief's position is not fully settled or regularized shows that the institution of the state is only partly developed. Other variations are easy to discern by examining the table.

Alterations in Power Patterns

It must not be supposed that the foregoing analysis is sufficient to provide the key to the mystery of historical change, even in the simplest societies. Many other variables are involved, for example: the size of the society, the degree of participation in decisions, geographic and climatic factors requiring adaptation, types of economy (partly dependent on geographic realities), proximity of neighboring groups of greater or lesser aggressiveness, internal changes of values in the society, special segmental interests (including access to values, hereditary or otherwise), and diverse technologies. The levels-of-action scheme, when used with variables like these, is a useful guide for analyzing power structures in the process of development. It will also have relevance to larger social aggregations, which will occupy our attention in the following chapter.

III

Legitimacy and Power Contexts

Every society has limits: limits of resources, population, neighbors, and interests. Over the years, typical cultural preferences for a way of life that seems "right" accumulate. These preferences, unique to each society, constitute its value system. It was pointed out in Chapter II that consensus on these values is a basis for the massive power of the people. Bertrand Russell refers to this as "traditional power" and writes that it "has on its side the force of habit; it does not have to justify itself at every moment, nor to prove continually that opposition is not strong enough to overthrow it." [1] In short, it has legitimacy.

[1] Bertrand Russell, *Power, A New Social Analysis,* p. 38 (New York, W. W. Norton, 1938).

Legitimacy and Coercion

Legitimate power is that type which is exercised as a function of values and norms acceptable in the society. Examples from everyday life include a father's power to punish his own child, a court's power to cite an individual for contempt, a priest's power to grant absolution, and a treasurer's power to collect dues from members of an association. Conversely, illegitimate power is exercised in violation of those values. Someone who bribes an official to secure immunity from arrest would, in the eyes of most people, be using illegitimate power; so, too, would an official who puts pressure on his subordinates to kick back part of their salary to him. Some values are granted greater approval by everyone than are other values, and the extent of the agreement on the same values may vary a great deal. Power, especially in diversified or complex societies, may range from legitimate to illegitimate forms.

Closely related to power is the quality of coercion. In its extreme form coercion is naked force or violence applied so as to cause damage or destruction; less extreme is the threat of force or violence.

At the non-coercive end of the scale such phenomena as majority vote, diplomacy, and propaganda are found. It is worth noting that in these non-coercive situations, sanctions remain in the background and are not called into play unless the power is resisted; in that case non-coercive actions are quite likely to be transformed into coercive ones. For this reason, force has been called the *ultima ratio.*

The transmutation may work in the opposite direction as well. When force totally replaces other dimensions of power, it eliminates the resources of reciprocity and cooperation. This inevitably breeds resistance which is then countered mechanically with another dose of force, eventually bringing a vicious circle of violence into play. "Consequently any social system that depends mainly on force . . . is in a precarious position, for in the process of change this generated resistance is apt to find some opportunity to overthrow it."[2] Talleyrand's famous aphorism, "Sire, you can do everything with bayonets except sit on them," indicates that naked force has decided limits.

Both extremes of the coercive-non-coercive scale are unstable; there seems to be a movement of power relations toward the middle range. With non-coercive forms like majority vote, any challenge or resistance is apt to precipitate the calling out of police or military troops to enforce the decision. Conversely, the use of terror alone may prove so inefficient that appeals to non-coercive forms like tradition, patriotism, and supernatural sanctions become necessary. In other words, a plurality of power resources forms a more stable structure than a single resource.

It is possible to arrange the qualities of power along two axes: legitimacy-illegitimacy, and coercion-non-coercion. This is symbolized in Figure 5.

Figure 5 is self-explanatory. The four sectors are separated by double lines to indicate that sharp distinctions are often impossible and that there are doubtful or

[2] R. M. MacIver and Charles H. Page, *Society, An Introductory Analysis,* p. 157 (New York, Rinehart & Co., 1949).

Figure 5

The Dimensions of Power

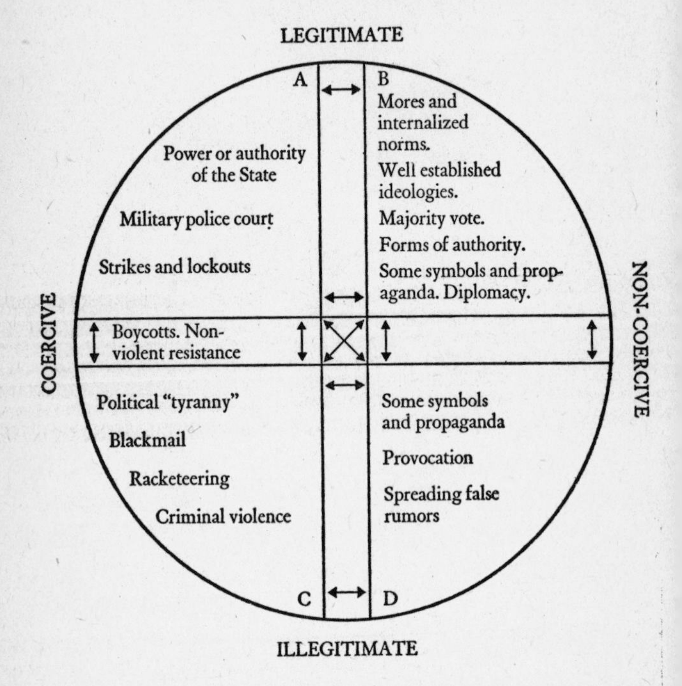

Sector A — Legitimate and coercive
Sector B — Legitimate and non-coercive
Sector C — Illegitimate and coercive
Sector D — Illegitimate and non-coercive

marginal cases such as boycotts. Such instances will depend for their resolution on the social context.

One feature of Figure 5 needs elaboration. The diagram as it stands is appropriate to a relatively stable society with fairly wide consensus on values and with some sort of "representative" government. A colonial area, on the other hand, lacks this sort of balance. Such a society with its different power relations would also have different legitimacy patterns as well. From the point of view of the people governed, Sector C (illegitimate and coercive power) might be overwhelmingly large. The vertical lines would shift to the right and the horizontal lines would move upward. The view of the colonizing power, however, would be much like that of the original Figure 5. When the two views are incongruous, misunderstandings, disagreements, and clashes arise in the struggle between two ways of life and two value systems in that struggle. Power relations are colored by the contrasting views of legitimacy.

The fact that Figure 5 can be redrawn to fit different social contexts illustrates the relativity of power arrangements. Of course it would be convenient if there were only one set of these patterns to show inherent stability; it might be tempting to think that Figure 5 could be a working model for all social systems so that all variations from it would be, by definition, unstable. But social realities are not so neatly arranged. There are some societies with many patterns of coercion and others where they are few; there are some cultures where illegitimate modes of action would seem to us to be dangerously numerous, and others where they are almost non-existent. Yet the consensus on the ratio between legitimate and illegitimate forms of power (different, let us say, from our own) might be quite overwhelming, and this consensus would ensure the stability of such a society.

The variations in legitimacy patterns depend not only on the nature of the value systems involved, but also on the degree of the rigidity of the society.

Rigid and Flexible Societies

The arrangement and disposition of segmental power structures in a society gives it a special character. It is highly instructive to observe diverse forms of social organization since they are so decisive in determining the processes and directions of social change. Focusing on the underlying forces that define and qualify every sort of rule adds a great deal to the traditional approach of classifying governments. For example, both Great Britain and Saudi Arabia are catalogued as monarchies, but to rank them together on this basis is hardly sufficient for power analysis. A more fruitful approach is to regard societies in terms of the rigidity of their power structures.

Societies with flexible power structures have one or more of the following characteristics: (1) separation or relative autonomy of the segmental power structures; (2) permissiveness allowing the formation of multiple voluntary associations; and (3) considerable mobility between or within occupational and class structures. The first feature appears to be more crucial than the other two.

Societies with rigid power structures, on the other hand, are marked by (1) consolidation of the power structures into a single ruling center; (2) inhibition of plural associations independently organized; and (3) highly restricted social mobility. Breaks in the third pattern occasionally appear when members of the upper strata single out individuals from below for "promotion" or where persons force their way up through intrigue and violence.

It goes without saying that no society is totally rigid or

completely flexible: these are only limits. This analytical scheme, however, makes it possible to compare the organization of power among different peoples separated by space, time, and historical development. It cannot, of course, be a substitute for the patient tracing in detail of the unique way in which, say, the Assyrian empire, the Greek city-state, the Roman republic, or the French monarchy came into existence—a task for which only the specialized historian has the training and aptitude. On the other hand, by focusing on the crucial factor of power, the scheme furnishes a conceptual tool that may prove useful to the historian as well as the political scientist, sociologist, and anthropologist.

Before applying and illustrating how this typology can be used, another word about the place of the state in the organization of power is in order. The proposition that the state embodies the military, economic, traditional, ideological, or other forms of power already pervasive in the society is now basic in power theory; in the words of Lasswell and Kaplan, "Political power . . . is a complex form which presupposes always other forms of power . . . The 'power of the state' cannot be understood in abstraction from the forms of power manifested in various types of interpersonal relations."[3]

But this admonition—an important one, to be sure—should not be misconstrued to say that the state is merely a passive instrument of the different groups or institutions within the society. One implication of our analysis in the preceding chapter should now be stated clearly: the state develops, to a greater or lesser degree,

[3] H. D. Lasswell and A. Kaplan, *Power and Society, A Framework for Political Inquiry,* p. 85 (New Haven, Yale University Press, 1950).

what may be called cumulative autonomy. Once the governmental institution is formed, it begins to assert its own power through laws, decrees, and judicial or military decisions. In flexible societies the state is only one center of power in a plurality of centers; at times a *primus inter pares,* it has limited autonomy. In rigid societies the state commonly absorbs and concentrates most forms of power in its own action; thus it has wide autonomy. But there are exceptions to this general principle, namely when power is consolidated about some power structure other than the state. (Note the Latin American example below.)

One additional point: as the state develops autonomy, it absorbs and shapes other forms of power in its own way; these other power resources then become transmuted into the political form, which may now claim primary legitimacy in the social order. It then becomes necessary to speak of political power in addition to the military, economic, and religious forms already noted. Hermann Heller points out that ". . . a distinction should be drawn between state power and political power per se. For political power is exercised not only by the state but also by smaller political associations within it . . . churches, entrepreneur associations, trade unions and the like—which have no inherent political function. Not every political power as such is state power, but in the eyes of its incumbents, at least, every political power is potentially state power. The only way the minor power group can be certain of imposing its will on the common life of the population is through the achievement of the ultimate in power; namely, state power. For state power towers above the power exercised by smaller pluralistic groupings in that it controls the system of law which is set up and perpetuated by state organs."[4]

Political power, therefore, is either the power exercised by the state or that of a segmental power structure seeking incorporation in state action. The rise of the state tends to "politicalize" other power activities. Since the majority of early states came into being by conquest rather than by other means,[5] the coalescence of military and political power have been typical at one stage of society development. Even economic power, important as it is, was drawn in, since land was acquired by force during conquest. As Bertrand Russell has said, "Apart from the economic power of labor, all other economic power, in its ultimate analysis, consists in being able to decide, by the use of armed force if necessary, who shall be allowed to stand upon a given piece of land and to put things into it and take things from it."[6] The conclusion follows that the consolidation of power in early governments marks them as characteristically rigid in terms of the present analysis.

Power in Rigid Societies

A good many preliterate kingdoms of the more highly organized type have a rigid power structure. Among the Bantu of South Africa supreme power is concentrated

[4] Hermann Heller, "Power, Political," *Encyclopedia of the Social Sciences,* Vol. 12, p. 301 (New York, Macmillan, 1937). Used with the permission of the Macmillan Company.

[5] Ralph Linton, *The Study of Man,* pp. 240-243 (New York, D. Appleton-Century Co., 1936).

[6] Russell, op. cit., p. 120.

in a ruler who can say with far more justification than did Louis XIV, "L'état, c'est moi." The Bantu king legislates on his own; professional magicians and tribal doctors are his own specialists; he controls the distribution and use of land; grants or refuses permission for marriages; "controls" the rainfall; and is military chieftain in war.[7] A number of African societies—Dahomey, Ashanti, and the Zulu empire, for example—have been especially rigid in their power structure.[8]

Ancient civilizations such as Babylonia and Egypt united the major forms of power in the ruler of the state. This process was sometimes augmented by the necessity to control mass labor for vast irrigation projects requiring constant regulation. While the monarch at the apex of the system had almost unlimited power, the state constituted the bureaucratic apparatus for managing the dikes, keeping the channels open, regulating land use, collecting crops and taxes, defending the population, and extending the borders by military operations.[9]

Such centralized states eventually developed extensive secondary value systems: a specialized body of beliefs rooted in tradition but elaborated in myth and imagery into a sacred support for the system of rule. The function of maintaining the secondary value system was performed by a priestly class whose theological writings

[7] I. Schapera, *Government and Politics in Tribal Societies,* pp. 41-130 passim (London, Watts, 1956).

[8] M. J. Herskovits, *Dahomey, An Ancient West African Kingdom,* 2 vols. (New York, 1938); M. J. Herskovits, *Man and His Works, The Science of Cultural Anthropology,* pp. 333-338 (New York, A. A. Knopf, 1948); and E. A. Ritter, *The Rise of the Zulu Empire* (New York, G. P. Putnam's Sons, 1957).

[9] Karl Wittfogel, *Oriental Despotism, A Comparative Study of Total Power* (New Haven, Yale University Press, 1957).

and statements warranted the divine origin of the ruler.[10] A belief system of this sort, partly anchored in time-honored supernaturalism, partly imposed by revelation, took the place of the more massive consensus characteristic of simpler societies. This secondary value system is a type of "political formula," as Gaetano Mosca uses the term. Concerning such formulas, which in his view are a necessary basis of all political power, Mosca remarks that any criticism of them "does not mean that political formulas are mere quackeries aptly invented to trick the masses into obedience. The truth is that they answer a real need in man's social nature; and this need, so universally felt, of governing and knowing that one is governed not on the basis of mere material or intellectual force, but on the basis of a moral principle, has beyond any doubt a practical and real importance."[11] At times, this secondary value system appeared as a "benevolence myth" that pictured "the despotic order as fundamentally good—in fact, as the only reasonable and commendable system of government."[12] It is interesting to reflect on the similarities and differences between ancient and modern rigid societies in the application of this principle.

In our own day the most conspicuous examples of rigid societies are the totalitarian dictatorships, concentrating, as they do, economic, military, and police power as well as education and propaganda in the hands of an elite class of state officials. The distinction between state power and political power is all but obliterated; supreme

[10] Ibid, pp. 92-93.

[11] Gaetano Mosca, *The Ruling Class,* p. 71 (New York, McGraw-Hill, 1939).

[12] Wittfogel, op cit., pp. 134-135.

power is now political, drawing into its orbit the other forms of power. "Political power has at its command all instruments of economic power: the means of production, consumer goods, wages and prices."[13] It also has a complete monopoly of control over violence in its armed forces and, as a supplement, a vast network of secret police and informers to ferret out deviations and suppress them by terroristic means.[14] Ideological power, too, is subservient to the political: the state "has at its command all psychological means of coercion, i.e., propaganda and education . . . leisure time appears merely as a function of working time, and working time, in turn, as a function of political power . . . Culture is transformed into a commodity."[15] Separate or autonomous associations in the society are taboo; all are harnessed in the service of the political power. There is "synchronization of all social organizations—not only to control them, but to make them serviceable to the state."[16] The rise from lower to higher social positions is managed from above. Particularly with the advent of Stalin as the dominating leader in Russia, "the characteristic mode of selecting Party officials became designation from above rather than election from below."[17] The organization of power in totalitarian states seems to represent a more

[13] Franz Neumann, *The Democratic and the Authoritarian State,* p. 267 (Glencoe, Ill., The Free Press, 1957).

[14] Jerzy Gliksman, "Social Prophylaxis as a Form of Soviet Terror," *Totalitarianism,* Carl J. Friedrich, ed., pp. 60-74 (Cambridge, Mass., Harvard University Press, 1954).

[15] Neumann, op. cit., p. 267.

[16] Ibid, p. 245.

[17] Merle Fainsod, *How Russia Is Ruled,* p. 149 (Cambridge, Mass., Harvard University Press, 1953).

rigid pattern than can be found in earlier absolutist states or dictatorships; this fact has been attributed by some to the more efficient technological means at the disposal of communist or fascist states.[18]

An interesting variant of rigid power structure appears in many Latin American countries where economic power is predominant and the state is relatively weak. A handful of owners and managers control agriculture and mining which dominate the economy. In Chile 1.4 per cent of the landholdings account for 68.2 per cent of the farm area; in Brazil 1.5 per cent of the holdings incorporate 48.4 per cent of the farm area. Lack of crop diversification and dependence on world markets for the sale of a single commodity intensify this control. In Brazil 50 to 60 per cent of the value of exports comes from coffee; in El Salvador, Guatemala, and Colombia, this percentage rises to between 70 and 80. Where there is extensive mineral wealth, much of it is controlled by foreign capital, with the top echelons of management brought in from abroad. Most industrial production is relatively undeveloped.

Superimposed on this tight concentration of economic power is a "representative" political system where mass illiteracy restricts political participation for most citizens. It is impossible for the few upwardly mobile men to rise in either the agrarian or mineral fields and their opportunities to advance in industry are negligible. Their

[18] Friedrich, op. cit., pp. 53-56. For a comparison with earlier regimes see especially N. S. Timasheff, "Totalitarianism, Despotism, Dictatorship," *Totalitarianism,* op. cit., pp. 39-47; and Franz Neumann, "Notes on the Theory of Dictatorship," *The Democratic and the Authoritarian State,* op. cit., pp. 233-253.

main chances to move upward in the power system are in the army or the bureaucracy, both of which offer fairly low incomes but considerable prestige and at least access to wealth. The military proves to be the short-cut to governmental power, open to a *caudillo* with a loyal band of followers whom he can reward upon his accession to political office. Once in power, he retains his governmental position on the assumption that he will not disturb the economic equilibrium (the power of the large landowners). The narrow path to high position is confined by the rigid framework of the massive economic institution; circulation of political leaders in palace revolutions does not result in extensive social change. Under existing conditions it would be dangerous to disturb the realities of economic control since upheaval would not only threaten the positions of landholders and investors but also might result in widespread unemployment, poverty, and possible starvation for the masses immured in the system.

The rigidity of Latin American societies is therefore concentrated in the immobile and static economic sphere rather than in the state; the landowning class keeps a tight rein on political policy through protégés in government or by supporting one *caudillo* against another. The state is essentially an arena in which the avenues to power and status are narrowly restricted to those outside the well-entrenched and traditional power centers. Under such conditions, Pareto's "circulation of the elite" becomes a recurrent phenomenon except that these "circulators" belong to a secondary elite. Bolivia, for example, had nine revolutions in the ten years preceding 1951: not a single president served his full constitutional term during the years 1926-1951. Nearby Ecuador had fourteen presidents between 1931 and 1940, four of them during a single month ending September 17, 1947.[19]

Power in Flexible Societies

The chief characteristic of flexible societies is, by and large, the unevenness of power distribution: power is distributed to many centers. This feature is distinctive of most democracies from ancient Greek times to our own day. In Athens the public assembly alternated from one policy to another depending on circumstances: "In the fifth century the military officers, of whom the most important were the ten generals, were elected by the assembly. In the fourth, when finance became a difficult problem, a few high financial officers were also elected."[20] Periodic shifts from military to economic dominance were recurrent in Greek history, the Athenian democratic state becoming at times a tool, at other times a mediator, of segmental power structures.[21]

European feudalism is another notable example of a flexible power structure. In feudal society there were plural centers of power: the monarch with his court, the nobility of different grades, the church, and the commercial urban centers. The relation between a lord and

[19] This Latin American analysis owes indebtedness to Merle Kling, "Towards a Theory of Power and Political Instability in Latin America," *Western Political Quarterly* 9:21-36 (March, 1956).

[20] A. H. M. Jones, *Athenian Democracy,* p. 3 (New York, Frederick A. Praeger, 1958).

[21] See J. Penrose Harland, "From Kingship to Democracy" and George M. Harper, Jr., "Tyranny," *The Greek Political Experience, Studies in Honor of William Kelly Prentice* (Princeton, Princeton University Press, 1941).

his vassal was ambiguous since the latter was bound to conditional rather than unconditional service; the territory held in fief by the nobles was theirs to do with as they liked if they gave minimal loyalty, military service, or tribute to the lord from whom they received it.[22] The monarch's supremacy was often nominal because it was fiercely challenged and frequently nullified by pressures from the nobles, the church, and the commercial classes. The church did not depend solely upon supernatural sanctions but enjoyed temporal power in the form of vast estates and military forces that made archbishoprics into petty kingdoms.[23]

Here, only brief mention can be made regarding the important case of modern democratic societies. But it should be noted that most of them, which arose in the period of liberalism, eying the concentration of power in the state with distrust, not only limited governmental activities to a sort of minimal regulation, but separated and restricted various state functions. The multiple power centers in recent democratic societies have been given leeway to form and regroup themselves through frequent changes in the associational structure, while considerable mobility has continued. The power structure of democratic states took its form when economic power was shifting from landownership to commerce and small industry. "To these economic forces the liberal state guaranteed almost unlimited freedom of action . . . In the Middle Ages political power had to fight for its autonomy against religious power, while nowadays it has

[22] *The Sociology of Georg Simmel,* tr. and ed. by Kurt H. Wolff, pp. 210-211 (Glencoe, Ill., The Free Press, 1950).

[23] J. W. Thompson, *Economic and Social History of the Middle Ages (300-1300)*, p. 677 (New York, Century, 1928).

to struggle for it against economic power."[24] The resolution of this conflict still lies in the future. C. Wright Mills has presented a good deal of evidence to show that a shift toward rigidity has occurred in America,[25] a point that will occupy attention later in Chapter IV.

A final word about legitimacy. Rigid societies tend to be more monopolistic, deliberate, and manipulative about their principles of legitimacy, while flexibly organized societies depend as much on common consensus and traditional values as on "political formulas." This generalization has implications for the relations between power and social change.

[24] Hermann Heller, op. cit., pp. 303, 302.
[25] C. Wright Mills, *The Power Elite* (New York, Oxford University Press, 1956).

IV

Power and Social Change

Whenever men congregate there is movement, instability, restlessness. Social order seems to be more ideal than real. As Jules Henry, an anthropologist, has said, "If one assumes that society is inherently stable and orderly then the jolts and insecurities of contemporary life with all its disorderliness seem endlessly unexpected and disquieting, and one struggles ceaselessly to bring about an order, the exact nature of which it is difficult to discern. On the other hand, if one assumes that society is inherently unstable, then one accepts disorderliness as natural in a strict sense, and attempts to live in terms of perceived patterns of conflict and instability."[1]

If we assume that society is in a state of equilibrium determined by certain functional requirements, change,

[1] Jules Henry, "Homeostasis, Society and Evolution: A Critique," *Scientific Monthly* 81: 300-309, p 304 (December, 1955).

conflict, or power-encounters must be interpreted as "strains" or "stresses" which depart from an established firm position. (Terms like consensus, cohesion, and solidarity refer to this initial equilibrium.) Writers who start from this position are susceptible to a bias that prevents them not only from doing justice to social change but, in some cases at least, from treating adequately the positive value of change in social life because, whether they mean to or not, they tend to see society in static terms. In this chapter we shall take the opposite point of view, accepting change as a primary fact of our experience. Our study thus becomes the discovery of types of change and how they develop.

This is the framework of the present inquiry; our actual task, however, is much narrower. It is to examine the role of power in the initiation of change and will be a supplement to the familiar analysis that deals with such factors as geographical or climatic variations, migrations, industrial transformations, and technological inventions. An added advantage in studying power is that we come close to motivations found in everyday life. Bertrand Russell may have overstated his case but he undoubtedly was near the truth when he wrote, "love of power is the chief motive producing the changes which social science has to study."[2]

Power Distribution and Social Change

To go back to Bierstedt's concept of three sources of power cited in Chapter II: the various sub-units of any

[2] Bertrand Russell, *Power, A New Social Analysis,* p. 15 (New York, W. W. Norton, 1938).

society—and particularly the more complex ones—are marked by disparities in numbers, cohesive organization, and resources. It is highly unlikely that these sources of power would be identical in any two cases. Beginning with this premise, we can assume that at any point in time the actual state of affairs has been marked by an uneven distribution of power resources. This basic asymmetry is an essential human condition, a circumstance that sets the currents of social change in motion.

The unequal distribution of power serves as a spur to social activity in many different, and often contradictory, ways. It stimulates those with less power to increase their numbers, organization, or resources to a point where they can destroy the domination of an opponent and become dominant in turn, or to add resource to resource until they have power equal to the opponent, or to infiltrate the ranks of the adversary so as to share power with him ("if you can't lick 'em, join 'em"). It stimulates those with greater power to enlarge and extend their domination until it appears unshakable, to make concessions to the growing power of a weaker opponent in the hope that they will stem the tide, to attack the lesser power in the hope that direct attack will end the threat forever, or to employ indirect strategies that will in the long run weaken the power of the opponent.

The commitment of men to particular forms of legitimacy often determines the selection of methods. In cases where the goal is to share power with a ruling group rather than to dominate it, it is likely that the traditional value system either defines the ruling power as sacrosanct or views the excessive wielding of coercive power as an evil. In the former case, to upset the ruling power is a form of lese-majesty; in the latter case, usurpation is a violation of the pacific and harmonious way of life on which there is broad consensus. At times, both these tendencies appear in the same value system. The naked clash of will against will, too often presented as the typical form of power conflict, is far too simple to be satisfactory; yet from Thomas Hobbes in the seventeenth century to Karl Marx and the Social Darwinists in the nineteenth, this view has been advocated either implicitly or explicitly. Recognition of cultural variability in these matters is a relatively late development.

But there is this much truth in the simple power-clash theory. Fluid societies in rapid transition from one type of organization to another are marked by the breakup of traditional value systems, by anomie or normlessness, and thus the distinction between legitimate and illegitimate activities is blurred. Under these conditions, intrigue and coercion can easily displace other techniques of power; ethics and politics part company. Mass movements and enthusiasms can be easily aroused, charismatic figures rise to prominence, and novel utopian schemes become popular, as they did in the nineteenth century. The current of power can then flow more directly from the masses to the leader who in turn emboldens them, excites them, or gives them hope; old segmental power structures give way while new ones form rapidly. Force then comes into its own. Authority melts away.

Altering the Power Balance

Initiatory changes in the power structure proceed in two apparently opposite directions which may be termed briefly the enlarging and the supplanting of dominance.[3] Barrington Moore describes the enlarging process as follows: "The central feature of absolute monarchy is that the ruler of one segment of a large and loosely organized polity imposes himself upon and brings order to the larger group. Purely personal factors, such as the ambition of an able and energetic ruler, may under favorable circumstances be all that is required to start the process of acquiring power in the form of monarchical absolutism. Especially in its early stages, monarchical absolutism does not appear to be propelled forward by the deep tides of economic and social change. Once the process has begun, a tradition may be established that it is the duty of the monarch to expand and consolidate his authority through incorporating various classes and interest groupings in the service of the state."[4]

Supplanting of dominance is best exemplified by a revolutionary group or party whose aim is to seize power and set up a new rule. For this purpose the revolutionaries must create a new belief system opposed to the old, justifying discontent and promising a better life. They must organize a disciplined group but, most important of all, must center their attention on ways of weakening and destroying the old regime. Feliks Gross writes that at the time that the Russian Soviets made the final breakthrough in October 1917, "the blow, in the first stage, was concentrated against the *instruments* of power, not

[3] Dominance here refers to a condition where superior resources are concentrated in a unique power structure that makes it, for the time at least, a regnant force in the society or subsystem of a society.

[4] Barrington Moore, Jr., *Political Power and Social Theory*, p. 8 (Cambridge, Mass., Harvard University Press, 1958).

against its physical *symbols,* as the government buildings, and even the government itself. The Bolsheviks first seized the fortress and later the telegraph, telephone stations, power stations, the State Bank, and similar enterprises. Once the instruments of power had been captured, the government was doomed."[5]

The two types of power change are found in specific organizations as well as whole societies. Enlargement of dominance occurs when a corporation buys out a smaller company or when a dominant political party in a legislature gerrymanders a district to increase its voting strength. Supplanting of dominance also occurs in minor ways when a minority clique within management, disgusted with the methods of the executives at the top, starts a whispering campaign against them and finally buys a controlling share of stock to oust them once and for all.

Comparison of these methods shows that the enlarging of dominance concerns power centers in which the initiators are members; supplanting of dominance concerns those in which the initiators are not members of the regnant power structure. The process in the two cases has many similarities but the comparative emphases differ. In the first case, the initiators are more preoccupied with future gains and regard external obstacles as simply temporary hindrances to the attainment of their goals. In the second instance, their attention is focused on the destruction of obstacles, while the long-term gains frequently fade into an indefinite future outside the direct center of attention.

Either of these processes may provoke resistance and

[5] Feliks Gross, *The Seizure of Political Power in a Century of Revolution,* p. 229 (New York, Philosophical Library, 1958).

the active defense of the status quo by those who stand outside the initiators' immediate circle. This secondary or reactive power may in time develop its own impetus and display the same techniques that have been mobilized against it. It is useful to distinguish between the power acts of the initiators and those of the resistants: the former can be termed active power, the latter reactive. This distinction brings out the differences in time and highlights the derivative nature of reactive power. The distinction has, however, only limited validity: most forms of power are found to be reactive when their chronological sequence is traced.

The qualitative differences between the initiation of power processes by enlarging and by supplanting of dominance are summarized in Table B. It also shows

Table B

Variables in the Initiation of Power Changes

Variables of the process	*First Polar Opposite* (Enlarging of dominance)	*Second Polar Opposite* (Supplanting of dominance)
1. Value orientation	In line with the prevailing value system	In opposition to the prevailing value system A new legitimacy
2. Primary direction of attention	Toward value goal	Toward means for achieving goal (mobilization)
3. Techniques of attempted control	Facing inward Assimilation and absorption	Facing outward Methods of organization stressing policy, strategy, tactics
4. Power emphasis	Playing down of open opposition Concealment of aims The velvet glove Coercion only as last resort	More open opposition Concealment of aims a temporary strategy Greater willingness to use coercive means

what factors or variables may be combined in intermediate forms. Table B refers only to conscious and deliberate initiation of the power process; it excludes accidental initiation of power changes as well as the modifications that are unanticipated effects of other types of change.

Associations or organizations effecting minor changes in society will tend to display characteristics of the first polar opposite: enlarging of dominance. The more far-reaching the changes attempted, the more likelihood that the variables will be grouped around the other pole: supplanting of dominance. Table B is thus a useful model for analyzing groups or organizations seeking change; in such analysis it will be found that most groups occupy intermediate positions between the two poles with diverse combinations of the many variables. Quantification of the results can be obtained by discovering the amount of time the organization gives to each activity mentioned in Table B.

The initiation of change through the exercise of power is not an isolated process; when embodied in group activities, it becomes subject to the laws or tendencies of growing organizations. Philip Selznick has pointed out the paradox in large-scale organizations or bureaucracies: "Running an organization as a specialized and essential activity generates problems which have no necessary (and often an opposed) relationship to the professed or 'original' goals of the organization . . . 'Ultimate' issues and highly abstract ideas which do not specify any concrete behavior have therefore little direct influence on the bulk of human activities. This is true not because men are evil or unintelligent, but because the 'ultimate' formulations are not *helpful* in the constant effort to achieve . . . solutions to the specific problems which day-to-day living poses . . . Since . . . activities come to consume an increasing proportion of the time and thoughts of the participants, they are . . . *substituted* for the professed goals . . . In that conflict the professed goals will tend to go down to defeat, usually through the process of being extensively ignored."[6]

This trend is related to the second variable in Table B (primary direction of attention) and whether activity is pointed more to means than ends. Selznick and others call attention to the fact that growing organizations, by devoting so much time to means eventually lose sight of the ends. Longitudinal research on growing organizations, in which such changes over time are observed, would do much to extend our knowledge of power operations.

Power and Social Change in Three Types of Society

In earlier chapters are sketched the characteristic power structures of societies designated as participant, rigidly organized, and flexibly organized. In the first type power is massive and exercised primarily by a collective entity; in the second, power tends to be concentrated in a single individual, family, or tiny ruling clique operating through a state apparatus; in the third, power is diffuse and segmentally distributed throughout the social structure with the state having at least the nominally dominant position. The next question is: how is the transition made from one of these patterns to another?

[6] Philip Selznick, "An Approach to a Theory of Bureaucracy," *American Sociological Review* 8:47-54 (1943), quoted in *Sociological Theory, A Book of Readings,* Lewis A. Coser and Bernard Rosenberg, eds., p. 449 (New York, Macmillan, 1957).

A clue to the answer is found in Moore's proposition that "any society sooner or later falls victim to the limitations of its own success." [7] For purposes of this discussion we may add, "success in handling power."

In participant societies, value consensus is so pervasive that power struggles over community leadership are carefully played down; as long as power struggles do not harm the wider community, they are allowed on a segmental basis, that is, in the practice of private vengeance or family feuding. But massive control of individual behavior by the group is so strong, and the cultural consensus so compelling, that decisions about leadership are not left to competition or conflict between individuals; they are a matter of group decision. Intra-societal struggles for power are segregated from major group concerns, and in this way social change is kept to a minimum. The participant society is highly successful in maintaining control of its inner turbulence by strict primary group surveillance. This very success becomes a handicap under two conditions: when population growth enlarges the group so that lines of communication are weakened and the old controls break down; and when a perpetual state of warfare requires a hierarchy of command and obedience foreign to the society's way of life. The second condition is perhaps the more crucial one since the very techniques that serve so well in the internal environment make the tribe vulnerable to a highly organized attack. The helplessness of many sedentary agricultural peoples in the face of nomadic aggression with its unified leadership is a familiar feature of human history.

The solution to either or both of these problems requires an about-face in power organization: from a

[7] Barrington Moore, op. cit., p. 155.

diffuse to a concentrated form, from collectivity to hierarchy, from proto-democracy to kingship, from statelessness to the state. The first step away from the participant form seems to be a leap toward the rigid end of the scale. Although Leibnitz's assertion that nature never makes leaps may have been correct, it is hardly applicable to society. Slow, continuous change like that of population growth may lead, of course, to cumulative adaptive changes in the power structure so that a number of gradations will appear between a communal tribe and a tribe with a hereditary chieftain. But gradual development of this kind is only likely if, first of all, other factors remain constant and secondly if intelligent adaptations are carefully made at each step of the way. The probability that either of these conditions would hold in any single case is very small, although it cannot be ruled out completely. More probably the first assumption will be nullified by migration or invasion of other tribes into the area, and the second assumption canceled by the persistence of custom, which, in a period of change, may become maladaptation. Continuous maladaptation or neglect then results in a crisis where coercive measures are called for.

Participant (and other) societies are rarely presented with manageable problems one at a time, just as in a shop customers do not arrive singly at five minute intervals but come in bunches, followed by a lull in activity. In similar fashion, societies do not face single challenges at regular intervals but must cope with combinations or rapid successions of difficult situations. The conjunction of these situations in a crisis can precipitate the leap from one societal form to another. Such dramatic shifts illustrate the notion of historical dialectic made famous by

Hegel and Marx, at least in the first movement from thesis to antithesis.

Where conquest develops as the chief method of uniting peoples, rigid forms of control are widespread. Bertrand Russell remarks that "equal cooperation is much more difficult than despotism"[8] and that monarchies are the most common form of power structure throughout history. Concentration of power in the hands of the ruler and the ruling clique, formalized and channeled through state machinery, generates two major problems: (1) the need to decentralize so as to control regions at the periphery of the society or interest groups that must be satisfied to a considerable degree on their own terms; and (2) the need to assure loyalty to the ruler and his method of rule. Where the major economic, political, and military resources are monopolized by the chief or monarch and legitimacy is adequately buttressed by political formula, power conflicts are transmuted into rivalry for the attention and favor of the ruler. If he can keep separate segmental power structures from developing, there remains only his central one, which is so all-embracing that little room is left for power struggles except to fill the status positions within it. Social change may be rapid and intense in the upper ranks of the hierarchy, while the rest of the society retains a stable and traditional pattern of life. In outright despotisms this configuration is fairly common; usurpation is frequent; rivalry at the top is for total power with most other conflicts centering about incumbency for the higher positions. A variation of this pattern appears in the Latin American societies where concentration of power is outside the state proper.

[8] Russell, op. cit., p. 24.

Monarchical societies differ considerably in the degree of their rigidity. One major difference occurs with respect to the personal weakness of the rulers themselves which permits the growth of segmental power structures by default. This factor will come under scrutiny in the following chapter in the discussion of countervailing power.

Modern totalitarian societies with their extreme rigidity began with a great diversity of social elements which were methodically regularized. Arising from fluid conditions, both the Nazi and Communist parties established centralized authority by means of a state dictatorship. In Germany a highly productive economic system temporarily weakened by a depression was rejuvenated by the state by the simple expedient of channeling most manufacturing into armaments. In Russia, on the other hand, industry was not only imperfectly developed, but the dictatorship was bound by dogma and policy to assume responsibility for creating a new economic system. This self-imposed task of the Soviet dictatorship required much greater force and effort than that exerted by the Nazi leaders, who inherited an already well-developed economy.[9] In the Russian case, huge masses of men were compelled or manipulated into new patterns of life contrary to their habits and inclinations; they had to learn a new discipline as the fundamental avenue to economic survival, while the management of this vast enterprise was centralized in a bureaucratic state apparatus. The dictator and his hierarchy regarded themselves, however mistakenly, as the sole initiators of social change; they then scrutinized with suspicion any

[9] Franz Neumann, *The Democratic and the Authoritarian State,* p. 15 (Glencoe, Ill., The Free Press, 1957).

independent centers of power or influence and sought by every means to bring them into the orbit of state activity, or if this were impossible, to destroy them. By monopolizing economic, military, political, and propaganda resources, using all the technological aids of a scientific age, the dictator with his apparatus actually came very close to the ideal of initiating social change from a single center despite resistance among the peasants and industrial workers and despite internal struggles for power at the top, where legitimacy was not a settled issue but was often manufactured as the need arose.

The flexible organization of medieval society proved to be so unstable that it was later superseded by more centralized monarchical control. The nobles "managed to impose restraints upon both the prince and his councilors and executives. The organizational result of this extremely complicated, unresolved contest for supremacy was the gradual reconstruction of the central government on the basis of institutions, representative of the ruling groups, which were identical with the most affluent and most privileged elements of society. Thus, a sort of co-regency developed among the prince, the government bureaucrats, and the notables . . . Since these associations of local rulers were often divided by intergroup as well as intragroup quarrels, they held only an unstable share in the exercise of the central authority . . . Time and again, they wavered between organized cooperation and passive or active resistance. Their chief weapons were the techniques of political barter and contract which had developed within the feudal system. But when confronted with acute crises and sharp conflicts over the interpretation of customary law, the estates did not shun the use of violence . . . Such a federative government of ill-defined though constitutionally limited and divided powers was the typical basis of statehood throughout Europe from the thirteenth to the fifteenth centuries."[10] Much of the conflict so widespread in the Middle Ages arose from the clashing ideas of legitimacy rooted in the interests of disparate groups like the nobles, the church, the nominal ruler, and the commercial towns.

American society can be taken as a more recent representative of flexible organization, though this society is so many-sided that it is difficult to characterize it briefly. In America, political power was weakened from the outset by men reacting against absolutism and jealous of states' rights. The separation of governmental powers has created much internal struggle for dominance and the federal system has given considerable autonomy to geographic sub-centers. Another factor was the frontier spirit of pragmatism or getting things done by direct action in the economic sphere, a relentless drive that soon built up tremendous aggregations of wealth to challenge political authority in the making of social decisions. For a time sectionalism divided economic interests: "The cotton South vs. the dairying North, the agricultural-debtor West vs. the industrial-financial East."[11] Later, with the rise of giant corporations, clashes occurred at another level with coal arrayed against oil, railroads against airlines, mass buyers against mass producers, not to mention agriculture against labor. The extension of state activities that developed to regulate these inter-

[10] Hans Rosenberg, *Bureaucracy, Aristocracy and Autocracy. The Prussian Experience 1660-1815*, pp. 10-11 (Cambridge, Mass., Harvard University Press, 1958).

[11] Robin M. Williams, Jr., *American Society, A Sociological Interpretation*, p. 258 (New York, A. A. Knopf, 1951).

ests is sometimes interpreted to mean a massive increase in concentrated political power; but this view obscures the contrary possibility that the state is engaged in a huge balancing act in which the interests first of one sector in the economy, then another, are controlled or favored. Furthermore, "the growth of governmental regulation seems to stimulate the growth of the organization of private interests, and by that means, to increase the political strength of private groups."[12]

America is traditionally the land of associations—associations of businessmen, professionals, scientists, laborers, farmers, veterans, coreligionists, and many others. Each of these, under certain conditions, can become a pressure group attempting to influence political parties or the various centers of government. Since there are only two major parties, neither one can afford to alienate a substantial interest group permanently, nor can it identify itself too strongly with any one against an opponent. "Each party is a mélange of diverse economic interests, religious groupings, ethnic stocks, and so forth, and thus must compromise and integrate numerous conflicts in order to gain national power. The struggle for power therefore concerns immediate problems; conflicts cannot be brought to the sharp definition of irreconcilable principle without destroying party unity."[13] Alliances that shift from one election to another both reflect underlying changes in the society and determine further changes. Except during national emergencies, short-term concentrations of power and short-time policies seem to predominate. "The spirit of the party system deter-

[12] V. O. Key, Jr., *Politics, Parties, and Pressure Groups*, 3rd ed., p. 179 (New York, Thomas Y. Crowell Co., 1952).

[13] Williams, op. cit., p. 243.

mines the character of the government."[14] An executive strongly motivated to carry out a policy coming into conflict with his alliances, or those of legislators and administrative bureaus, will often appeal to the public directly for support. This technique is sometimes effective in spite of its demagogic implications, and in the hands of an effective propagandist, could eventually change the nature of political power itself.[15]

At present, however, social change in the power structure, to a very great extent, is a consequence of the strength, cohesiveness, and organization of multiple pressure groups interacting with each other, with political parties, and with government. Contextual forms of dominance are, of course, built up at times.[16] How they are counteracted is the theme of the next chapter.

[14] Norton E. Long, "Power and Administration," *Public Administration Review* 9 no. 4:257-264, p. 264 (1949).

[15] Ibid.

[16] This pluralistic picture of the American power structure stands in some contrast to that of C. Wright Mills, *The Power Elite* (New York, Oxford University Press, 1956), in which he portrays a consolidation of military, political, and economic power in the hands of decision makers drawn together by crisis conditions. For a thorough critique of Mills' position, see Daniel Bell, "The Power Elite—Reconsidered," *American Journal of Sociology* 64:238-250 (November, 1958).

V

Countervailing Power

Power has an inherent scarcity value. When one person or group gains more power, someone else has less. As MacIver and Page comment, "there are interests of *power* and *distinction* which by their very nature can be neither common nor harmonious. They cannot be harmonized because they are always *relative* to the possession of the power and distinction of others; these intangible goods cannot be apportioned in the same manner as can tangible goods. Thus a society can be ordered on the basis of equality of wealth, as in the case of some 'utopian' communities in modern times, but never on the basis of equality of power and prestige. There is no power where power is equal.[1] The quest for power and

[1] There is undoubtedly an abstract sense in which this proposition is valid but there are some difficulties in applying it concretely as is evident from the discussion of balance of power in Chapter I. For a relevant case of the balance of power between

distinction is unending in social life and is . . . a perpetual source of social conflict."[2] Every society therefore has dominant and subordinate power groups; the latter, with their disadvantaged position, can change the balance of power only through struggle and the appropriation of power from others, either by direct or indirect means. The exercise of power by such subordinate groups, particularly when they have positive gains to show, can be referred to as countervailing power.

This chapter illustrates briefly the drive for countervailing power in the following cases: the American Negro's struggle for higher economic and social status; organized labor's drive in the United States for a greater share in decisions affecting work; and the great shifts in power taking place in revolution exemplified by Russia.

The Changing Power Position of the Negro in America

The dominance of White over Negro in the United States was first institutionalized in slavery, a power relationship of continuous coercion embodied in both folkways and law. With the victory of the Union in 1865, the legal basis of race dominance was broken, and a regime of formal equality was imposed by the North upon the folkways of the South. Southern political turbulence combined with weariness in the North resulted in the withdrawal of federal troops from below the

two political parties, see H. P. Secher, "Coalition Government: The Case of the Second Austrian Republic," *American Political Science Review* 52:791ff. (December, 1958).

[2] R. M. MacIver and Charles H. Page, *Society, An Introductory Analysis*, p. 67 (New York, Rinehart, 1949).

Mason and Dixon line in 1877; many folkways of inequality were renewed and strengthened, although on a more informal level than before the Civil War. The economic depression of the 1890s created dislocation in the South; race feelings against the Negroes were intensified and the reaction against the colored population resulted in laws of segregation and disenfranchisement that established a semi-caste status for Southern Negroes. For almost twenty years lynchings and riots against Negroes—in the North as well as the South—took a heavy toll. When this type of violence reached Springfield, Illinois, the home of Abraham Lincoln, a reaction arose and the stage was set for a protest. In 1909 a new pressure group was born, the National Association for the Advancement of Colored People. Although other forms of countervailing power or pressure against White dominance have also appeared, their effectiveness and lasting influence have been minor compared with the NAACP and they cannot be considered here.

The value systems of South and North furnish the background of the power struggle. In the South, racism or the group-superiority motif is firmly embedded in folk beliefs as well as practices; segregation has come to be regarded by the White southerner as a permanent solution to racial strife, a symbol of order and stability in which he has a deep emotional involvement. As Thomas P. Bailey once put it, "The race attitude of the Southern Whites is not a code of cases but a creed of a people—a part of their morality and of their religion." [3] In the North, the value system is mixed and contra-

[3] Quoted in Alain Locke and Bernhard J. Stern, *When Peoples Meet,* p. 326 (New York, Progressive Education Association, 1942).

dictory. Humanitarian ideals and adherence to the Constitution furnish values of equal rights under the law while racism is a pervasive force remaining below the surface until called into play by circumstances usually involving racial contact. For this reason, people in the North are ambivalent in their attitudes toward Negroes; impersonal relations are frequently governed by equalitarian values, while personal relations are not. This confusion or conflict of values and the relative unimportance of segregation in the folkways account in large part for the average citizen's lack of awareness of the power dimension in race relations. Under such conditions, pressure group tactics, when applied to public opinion, political parties, and the organs of government can have considerable effect in increasing the Negro's rights. The greater use of the ballot by Negroes in the North is a pivotal factor in this process.

Where countervailing power arises, the subordinate group is more likely to be successful when the dominant group is divided in its opinions, strategies, organization, or resources. This is the situation in the North where the Whites have lacked cohesiveness vis-à-vis the Negroes (in stark contrast to the South); divided in opinion, they have acted haphazardly in formulating policies in race relations; many have shown considerable benevolence toward the Negro's claim to greater social equality. This internal split among Northern Whites is well illustrated by the origins of the NAACP which was first formed entirely of White citizens outraged at the increasing violence against Negroes. The Whites who called the first meetings then invited a group of Negroes to join with them in programs designed to change conditions. The organization, with its early interracial composition, did not become predominantly Negro at the policy-making level until the 1930s.

Adopting pressure group tactics, the NAACP launched its campaign to increase civil rights for Negroes and exerted its influence on public opinion, legislative bodies, administrative agencies, and the courts. The Association lays great stress on strategy and tactics, mobilizing of action in a boycott here, a lobby there, a well-placed lawsuit where major publicity for the cause can be obtained, and, at times, mass demonstrations—all planned for major impact on public opinion and governmental action. Although its membership has never equaled a tenth of the Negro population (and has actually declined since World War II), this minority representation within a national minority is characteristic of other American pressure groups; it is not too great a handicap, especially when coalitions with other libertarian organizations add strength to NAACP demands. The Negro's gains in public transportation, public accommodations, employment, housing, and education are not adequately explained as the result of NAACP activity, to be sure, but it seems probable that without the initiation of action and the unremitting pressure exerted by this militant organization, these changes would not have been effected.

Especially significant are the constitutional battles in federal courts. The NAACP won thirty-four out of thirty-eight cases before the Supreme Court even before the famous decisions on desegregation in education of 1954 and 1955.[4] The federal courts are important for they call into play governmental sanctions for enforce-

[4] Warren D. St. James, *The National Association for the Advancement of Colored People, A Case Study in Pressure Groups,* p. 130 (New York, Exposition Press, 1958).

ment that reach into the South through the exercise of federal power and thus affect public transportation, the franchise, and education. Because the challenge to segregation in education has potential far-reaching influence on the folkways of the entire South, it raises the question of the limits of federal power with great force in the United States.

The Changing Power Position of Labor in America

The case of labor relations offers an interesting contrast: altering the power balance between worker and management eventually requires more widespread social change than is sought by the NAACP, which affects chiefly, though not exclusively, the lives of a minority. Labor's struggle affects a larger segment of the population, and the changing balance between agriculture and industry has made it a crucial issue for more and more people since the 1890s. Another important difference is that labor's chief tactical weapon against the employer—the strike—is a blunt instrument that can not be wielded against management alone; in the case of nationwide strikes particularly it also inflicts damage or inconvenience upon a larger public and can easily alienate sections of it from labor's cause. Defiance of public opinion is a perennial calculated risk for organized labor. It should be noted too that the gaining of power by organized labor is highly dependent on the upward movement of the business cycle; at such times it is more necessary to press the demands of labor to meet the higher costs of living while the prospects of ready profits dispose the employer to make concessions. Such conditions are lacking during depressions.

In a rapidly expanding country marked by large-scale and long-range immigration, the employer enjoys a dual advantage in his conflict with labor: there is a fairly dependable pool of workers on which he can draw in case of emergency and the presence of different ethnic groups enables him to play off one against the other to his benefit. He is aided in this process "by competition and a continuous displacement in industry of nationalities of a high standard of living by those of a lower one."[5] The prevalent value system, with its emphasis on individual rights, individual self-determination, and equality of opportunity, codified in the documents of the Founding Fathers, favors employers. The expanding frontier also furnished some opportunities for at least a few of the frustrated or discontented, while continuing possibilities for starting small businesses attracted a steady stream of recruits from low-paid occupations. On the other hand, the doctrine of political equality gives an advantage to labor, but this doctrine was not interpreted in economic terms until relatively late in American history.

Under these conditions it has been a highly difficult task for labor not only to make economic gains but to establish itself as a distinct entity. Before machine industry was extensively developed, only skilled artisans had the cohesion of "equal financial endurance and of identical interest"[6] to maintain the kind of disciplines

[5] Selig Perlman, *A History of Trade Unionism in the United States,* p. 66 (New York, Macmillan, 1923).

[6] Ibid, p. 123.

needed to withstand wage pressures or withdraw their scarce skills from small employers when they might win substantial local victories. When industry burgeoned in the late 1880s, the mass organization of the Knights of Labor was formed, but numbers alone proved to be inadequate. Diffusion of membership in a large, unwieldy organization results in lack of discipline, solidarity, and strong leadership, a deficiency that proves fatal in a time of crisis. A show of force on the part of management when opposed by a weakly united labor association nearly always results in violence,[7] which can then be made the occasion for an organized drive against labor by employers who enlist the sentiments of the community for law and order. Employer retaliation of this kind was so effective in the 1880s that the Knights of Labor collapsed; only the unions of skilled workmen weathered the severe depression of the 1890s to form the nucleus of a lasting labor movement.[8]

The major task of organized labor has been, perhaps, the winning of public recognition—legitimation. As noted above, the value system of American society is strongly individualistic and middle class; the Constitution, too, embodies the values of individual and property rights. Thus the sporadic and often bloody gains of labor until World War II were frequently nullified by court decisions and legislative setbacks. Although court recognition that organized labor is not a conspiracy was made as early as 1842, the effects of this decision dissolved when conspiracy was freshly interpreted as a civil wrong

[7] Eugene V. Schneider, *Industrial Sociology,* p. 284 (New York, McGraw-Hill, 1957).

[8] Perlman, op. cit., Chapters 5 and 6.

rather than a criminal offense in 1893.[9] At the same time, courts imposed heavy financial and other penalties on the leaders of strikes and boycotts so that labor was stimulated to transfer much of its power struggle into the political sphere. On the whole, however, political action proved quite ineffective up to 1914 and resulted in the policy of punishing enemies and rewarding friends—a rather feeble weapon without the voting strength to reinforce it.

Labor's battle for legitimation was given new strength by two major socio-economic changes. The first of these occurred in World War I when, under the pressures of military emergency, the federal government embarked on a new policy to ensure labor's cooperation with the war effort; this included granting the right to bargain collectively and admitting labor leaders to high policy-making positions in administrative agencies. The second major change came in the depression of the 1930s when under the New Deal a Congress friendly to labor enacted a bill establishing the right to organize (the Wagner Act, 1935) and created the National Labor Relations Board to supervise the Act's provisions, especially those devoted to bargaining collectively in good faith."[10] During World War I organized labor increased its membership by three quarters of a million; in the 1930s the newly formed CIO (as well as elements of the older AFL) continued more successfully the organization of unskilled, industry-wide unions attempted so many years before by the Knights of Labor. With the legal right to organize established, the CIO gained large

[9] Ibid, p. 158.
[10] Schneider, op. cit., pp. 230-231.

numbers of adherents in the steel, automobile, and rubber industries; part of this triumph may have been due to a new and somewhat quixotic tactical weapon, the sit-down strike. By occupying the plants of a company, strikers thus prevented the use of violence against themselves. Paradoxically, this new weapon was declared illegal by the courts after the battle had been won in the plants.[11] Large gains had been made, however, and they were augmented by a resurgence of labor during World War II. The two world wars and the New Deal reaction to the depression, then, provided periods of rapid social change in which labor extended its power by the use of previously inaccessible resources.

In time the labor-management conflict shifted more and more to the arena of government as the mediator of pressures and counter-pressures. As the courts became more amenable to labor's appeal to the general welfare clause of the Constitution, employers shifted their attack to the legislative branch. Eventually the Taft-Hartley Act of 1947, which reduces the power of unions in important respects, was passed. Whether in retaliation or not, the AFL and the CIO merged in 1955, uniting the forces of labor for a more unified program. Investigation of corruption in labor unions, on the other hand, led Congress in 1959 to pass the Labor-Management Reporting and Disclosure Act as a corrective of certain abuses in the labor movement. In so doing it singled out labor organizations as subject to regulations not applied to other voluntary organizations.[12]

[11] Ibid, p. 234.

[12] Joseph E. Finley, *Understanding the 1959 Labor Law,* pp. 11-13 (Washington, Public Affairs Institute, 1960).

Today the terms Big Labor and Big Business sometimes give the impression that equalization of power between the contestants has occurred. This is something of an overstatement. Although nationwide bargaining takes place in the larger industries, only about one-third of the nonagricultural labor force is organized;[13] assuming that one of labor's major goals is complete unionization, this would bring it far short of its aim. The effect of unions on wages, hours, and so-called fringe benefits is greater than this minority showing would indicate, however, since non-union firms competing for labor often keep their rewards high to avoid losing workmen to unionized plants. It is not impossible that the power of unions in the United States will stabilize around this pace-setting position without advancing any farther. American values still allow for toleration of unions on a rather grudging basis; public opposition is no longer directed at the legitimacy of labor organization but rather at its abuses. Privately, and in the folkways, disfavor is widespread. This situation parallels that of Negro-White relations.

Revolutions

Revolutions differ from the other two examples of countervailing power in several ways: (1) they seek displacement rather than equalization of power; (2) they alter the basis of legitimacy (that is, the value system); (3) social change in a revolution is massive and pervasive,

[13] *Directory of National and International Labor Unions in the United States,* Bulletin 1267, U. S. Department of Labor (Washington, 1959).

affecting an entire society rather than segmental portions of it; (4) because of revolution's wider scope, coercion and violence are standard features used both to destroy the old regime and to keep the new one in force.

In the Russian case, which will be the main example here, the monarchy in the early twentieth century was rigidly despotic. Supported by the aristocracy and in league with the church, it ruled with an iron hand. "Russian autocracy provided no instrumentalities for an open and legal struggle to that end" (a republic).[14] Rulers supported the privileges of the aristocracy thus binding them by favors. Compared with the rest of Europe, Russia was imperfectly industrialized with a poorly developed middle class. Most capital was supplied from abroad, many of the industries and utilities were state managed, and the state bank controlled the entire credit system.[15] Industrial workers had almost no rights of assembly, election, or discussion of political issues before 1905; the government even gave the police the task of organizing unions, thus assuring control.[16] There was practically no independent peasantry; the measure providing for the emancipation of the serfs in 1861 looks harsh to present-day eyes—it allowed a peasant to buy land only with the consent of his landlord, and to have full title only when all other members of the village had it. Peasants were thus stripped of economic power

[14] Feliks Gross, *The Seizure of Political Power in a Century of Revolutions,* p. 4 (New York, Philosophical Library, 1958).

[15] Ibid, p. 25.

[16] Karl Wittfogel, *Oriental Despotism, A Comparative Study of Total Power,* pp. 180-181 (New Haven, Yale University Press, 1957).

and, without the franchise, lacked political power as well. The army, recruited from peasants and workers, was "not imbued with the spirit of self-conscious modern nationalism which would make them willing to bear for long the terrible sacrifices demanded by war."[17] Both in the Crimean and the Russo-Japanese wars, the military services displayed internal weaknesses predictive of serious rupture.

In 1905 Russia experienced a massive dress-rehearsal of its final revolution. Discontent was widespread after the debacle of the Russo-Japanese War. Aroused to complain and demand redress from grievances, a party of workers with a political petition, led by Father Gapon of the Orthodox Church, approached the Tsar's palace where many were shot down before their cause was heard. This event inflamed St. Petersburg; mobs formed in the streets and the city took on the appearance of an armed camp; demonstrators were again met with fusillades. While this uprising of January eventually died down, a new one arose in October, rapidly expanding into a general strike. The workers' demands began with economic issues but eventually took on political forms. This time the Tsar promised civil rights and the establishment of a representative legislature (the Duma). Fundamental laws (consisting of a constitution) were granted but later, as the excitement died down, the Tsar dismissed one Duma after another and reduced the franchise of both workers and peasants. At the time of the Tsar's first capitulation, workers in St. Petersburg elected a council (Soviet) which captured the

[17] Hans Kohn, "Russian Revolution," *Encyclopedia of the Social Sciences,* Vol. 8, p. 477 (New York, Macmillan, 1937).

loyalties of the strikers and served as a new center of power for two months, after which its members were arrested. This pattern reappeared later.

While a few constitutional reforms were won in 1905, the revolution was abortive since the masses gained no real access to institutional power. It failed to enlist the peasantry and was almost strictly an urban workers' movement. The Tsar, however, lost the confidence of his people in 1905 and the legitimacy of his reign came into serious question.

In 1917 the final revolution took place. It occurred in two stages—a spontaneous uprising in February and a planned coup in October. In the background of the former was, once again, a luckless war effort. Combat against Germany resulted in a million and a half deaths in the field and mass desertion of nearly as many troops; hunger, inflation, and the rigors of winter led to widespread desperation and revolt in the capital. Mass strikes began and at first were dispelled by royal troops. The Tsar, overconfident, dissolved the Duma and thus created the first symbol of the revolution. This action precipitated a mutiny in the army regiments, who marched on the Tauride Palace, seat of the Duma, gathering an immense crowd of workers on the way. Placing themselves at the disposal of Kerensky, the troops recognized his authority rather than that of the Tsar. The provisional committee of the Duma, by now the sole ruler of Russia, assumed control.

With the new freedom of assembly a workers' Soviet formed again in St. Petersburg and later in other cities. During the eight months from February to October, the Soviet became an increasingly strong and independent center of power; it took over control of post offices, railroad stations, police, and communications systems, as well as a growing number of military forces in the capital city. Because the provisional government was occupied with constitutional questions and the continued prosecution of the war, the Soviet assumed many of these important operations by default. Within the Soviet, a well-organized minority party (Bolsheviks), unified and disciplined under the leadership of Lenin, agitated persistently for an end to the war, the withdrawal of support from the provisional government, confiscation of land with redistribution to the peasants, and the establishment of a private army, the Red Guard.

Not only did the Bolshevik party gain control of the Soviet, but by fraternizing with soldiers and sailors, its members won their confidence. While the provisional government lost power because of its unpopular decision to carry on the war and its vacillation on the land question, the Soviet won more and more solid support from workers, soldiers, and sailors. By October, Lenin, now in supreme command of the Soviet, decided that the time was ripe for a coup to be carried out by the military leaders Trotsky and Antonov. As described in Chapter IV, the Red Guard and the Military Revolutionary Committee together with a few military regiments and armed Bolsheviks seized the technological apparatus of the city along with the fortress and government buildings. No mass uprisings occurred, but the general confusion was an appropriate setting for decisive action. The provisional government, now powerless, abdicated. Revolutionary Soviet leaders captured the power of the Russian state for their own.

What does this all-too-brief sketch of the revolution in Russia tell us about countervailing power? It suggests that the process of power transfer on a revolutionary scale requires—or at least is greatly abetted by—specific conditions. The first of these is an incubation period in which the access to power by an increasing number of groups or classes is blocked; at such a time there is an erosion of the value system and widespread questioning of legitimacy. The second condition is a crisis situation in which a sharp rise of tensions in the populace coincides with a state emergency ineptly handled. Military forces become divided or change allegiance at this time. Finally a planned uprising or coup takes place, spearheaded by decisive leaders whose bold actions, backed by force of arms, topple the waning power of the old regime.

De Jouvenel's comment on revolutions is not far amiss: "The cycle began with the downfall of an inadequate Power only to close with the consolidation of a more absolute Power." [18]

Our entire study, so far, has dealt with power in the context of whole societies. The discussion would be incomplete, however, without some attention to smaller social units, and therefore we turn in the final pages from the macroscopic to the microscopic in order to explore the issue of power in the local community.

[18] Bernard de Jouvenel, *On Power, Its Nature and the History of Its Growth*, p. 216 (New York, The Viking Press, 1949).

VI

Power in the Local Community

We turn in this chapter to more familiar ground. Every reader has at least a passing acquaintance with the leaders, party politics, and community issues and ways of deciding them in his own city, town, or village. Sociological analysis of community power relations should then throw some light on his interpretation of local events.

Social research on the power structures of local communities is somewhat more advanced than inquiry into the national patterns. Though not yet detailed enough to supply answers to many specific questions, these findings nevertheless suggest an outline the details of which can be specified locally. The following review will focus on four major themes: governmental versus non-governmental controls, patterns of power distribution, selection of issues for decision-making, and role images of leaders.

Governmental versus Non-governmental Controls in the Community

In every town or city certain decisions are made outside the city council or mayor's office, others are referred to the government only when they have substantial support, and still others at least appear to be initiated and carried through by government personnel alone. It is hard to be sure that decisions of the last type are not the result of invisible community pressures.

Arthur Vidich and Joseph Bensman speak of the "minimal non-surrenderable functions of police control, street maintenance, water supply and elections" as areas where publicly visible decisions are absolutely required.[1] At the same time, many decisions appear to be made by extra-governmental means while the government plays the role of registering those that require political action to make them legal. At the informal or non-governmental level, leaders, cliques, and associations exercise power through networks of social groupings that form temporary alliances or, in other cases, more permanent coalitions. Some of these may include members of the city council or the mayor so that networks of communication are constantly kept open.

These informal clusters of power may have their source of legitimacy in the folkways, some of which may be unique to the community. As J. S. Coleman remarks, "the outcome of one dispute loads the dice in favor of a similar

[1] Arthur J. Vidich and Joseph Bensman, *Small Town in Mass Society: Class, Power and Religion in a Rural Community*, p. 135 (Princeton, Princeton University Press, 1958).

outcome the next time. Only a few such incidents may be necessary to fix the path of community disputes for fifty or a hundred years to come."[2] However, research is still needed to determine whether the sources of legitimacy are community-wide or whether they are restricted to limited groups whose prestige or coerciveness enables them to impose their views upon others. Further probes are also required to discover whether legitimacy in the community is restricted to highly limited spheres of decision-making. There probably is a good deal of variability from one community to another on such matters.

A pervasive value-system may reflect the national ethos and affect many communities. American individualism, for example, commands widespread attachment in the United States. One feature of individualism, the priority of informal over formal controls, forms the motif of freedom and laissez-faire in social life by tending to establish extra-governmental forms of activity as preferable to governmental action. As Robin Williams puts it, "a major implicit cultural premise in the dominant valuation of freedom has been the equating of freedom with control by diffuse cultural structure rather than by a definite social organization. Thus it has seemed to make a great difference whether the individual receives a certain income or has a certain type of occupation as a result of impersonal, anonymous, diffuse competitive process as against being forced to accept that employment or remuneration by law or by the command of a visible social authority."[3]

[2] James S. Coleman, *Community Conflict,* p. 2 (Glencoe, Ill., The Free Press, 1957).

[3] Robin M. Williams, Jr., *American Society, A Sociological Interpretation,* p. 419 (New York, A. A. Knopf, 1951).

In like fashion, individualism, growing out of the American experience of subduing the wilderness, exploiting the vast resources of a continent, and establishing new communities where none had been before, relegated the task of social coordination to the background of attention. Government, often enough, became an afterthought, subordinate to the "real" concerns of men, which were largely economic. In many ways legitimacy for government became ceremonial and symbolic while business and agriculture attained a higher value priority.

Local communities reflect these individualistic values when they choose community leaders who are not political officials to make weighty decisions. Vidich and Bensman document this pattern for a rural village in upstate New York and they speak of the invisible government.[4] Floyd Hunter reports that in a large Southern city, a small number of influential citizens dominate community policy-making by acting in concert through informal business cliques while political leaders occupy lower echelons of power.[5] Norton Long, in a study of several metropolitan centers, maintains that when the press and broadcasters ask for leaders to solve crises, their demand is for private rather than official public leaders. In his judgment, when citizens posit the existence of such leaders, this action furnishes them with a kind of psychic security which fills the vacuum left by the absence of the more absolutistic rulers of the past. The mass media often credit such informal leaders with both running things and neglecting things; "the idols are both worshipped

[4] Vidich and Bensman, op. cit., pp. 146ff.

[5] Floyd Hunter, *Community Power Structure, A Study of Decision-Makers,* pp. 62, 90ff. (Chapel Hill, N. C., University of North Carolina Press, 1953).

and beaten, at least verbally . . . This belief in part creates the role of top leadership and demands that it somehow be filled."[6] Vidich and Bensman comment similarly on a dominant leader behind the scenes in Springdale: "All groups and individuals over-estimate his authority, but by this very fact they increase his power since they act on the basis of their estimation."[7]

Research has established the fact that the top leaders in the informal structure are likely to be businessmen. Delbert Miller makes this point clear by comparing the nature of leadership in American and English communities. His study shows that business leaders form 67 per cent of the key influentials (those at the apex of the power structure) in Pacific City, 75 per cent in the Southern metropolis studied by Hunter, but only 25 per cent in a comparable English city. In the latter, professional persons in education, religion, civic organizations, and cooperatives, as well as prominent figures in trade unions and the Labor Party are abundantly represented; the English city has a more diversified group of leaders than is characteristic of the American communities studied.[8]

Although it is yet uncertain how widespread the pattern is, the American communities that have been carefully investigated show a decided preference for non-governmental controls, private rather than official

[6] Norton E. Long, "The Social Community as an Ecology of Games," *American Journal of Sociology* 64:251-261, pp. 255-256 (November, 1958).

[7] Vidich and Bensman, op. cit., p. 277.

[8] Delbert C. Miller, "Decision-Making Cliques in Community Power Structures: A Comparative Study of an American and an English City," *American Journal of Sociology* 64:299-310 (November, 1958).

leaders, and business leaders rather than men from other occupations. These findings require independent verification for other communities and must be balanced by inquiry into the way power structures are organized.

Patterns of Power Distribution

Is there a typical "shape" for the power structure in American communities? It has been common for students of the problem to think of such a pattern as a pyramid having a small oligarchy of highly influential leaders at the top, a larger group of lesser figures at middle levels, and numerous followers at the base. Hunter's study undoubtedly did much to disseminate this view since he pictured a group of financial and corporation executives in Regional City at the apex of power, with their decisions possessing great weight even though such men had no formal authority. Policy decisions were made in private sessions and passed down to the second echelon of power (professional and political leaders) where a larger group of subordinates mobilized public opinion on behalf of policies already adopted. Being assured of support from the top echelons, secondary leaders were usually quite successful in carrying out the plans already formulated. Although Hunter disclaims the use of the pyramidal pattern, students of his findings conclude that it is difficult to interpret his research conclusions in any other way.[9]

Subsequent studies have shown wide differences in

[9] Herbert Kaufman and Victor Jones, "The Mystery of Power," *Public Administration Review* 14:205-212, p. 207 (Summer, 1954).

community power distribution. Roland J. Pellegrin and Charles H. Coates report, for example, that the leaders of Bigtown, a Southern city of 200,000 population, spoke approvingly of Regional City (the scene of Hunter's research) where things were "done right" and a small compact group "controls civic affairs with a firm hand." The same Bigtown leaders were pessimistic about their own community, deploring its lack of unity, the conflict between business cliques, and the failure to carry out many plans of community development.[10] On the basis of Pellegrin and Coates's observations, Bigtown appeared to have not a pyramidal or hierarchical pattern but a series of elongated, finger-like structures extending downward from upper levels of power.

The studies of Robert Schulze, C. W. M. Hart, and James McKee reveal power configurations of even greater diversity. Schulze investigated an industrial suburb where major industrial plants had been absorbed by absentee-owned corporations. The managers of these plants maintained a strictly hands-off policy in local affairs, leaving their direction to men who were not economic dominants.[11] This neglect appeared to leave a unique power vacuum at the top where several large companies were involved. It seemed that local managers did not agree on this permissive policy beforehand but adopted it singly in response to national company directives separately issued. These different directives converged in the local community.

[10] Roland J. Pellegrin and Charles H. Coates, "Absentee-Owned Corporations and Community Power Structure," *American Journal of Sociology* 61: 413-419 (March, 1956).

[11] Robert O. Schulze, "Economic Dominants in Community Power Structure," *American Sociological Review* 23:3-9, pp. 6-8 (February, 1958).

It is quite obvious that policies made outside the community narrow the range of decisions made within it, or, in extreme cases, determine what will be done locally. Roland Warren, whose provisional study of this problem has opened up important avenues for exploration, shows the existence of various types of control from outside the community—informal control through culture patterns and formal control through governmental regulations at the state level affecting taxation and education, working conditions, and wage deductions. Frequently there are economic units that are parts of organizations, which set forth policies or regulations to govern operations of these units in each city or town. Finally there are national or international organizations, such as the Red Cross, American Legion, and the Roman Catholic Church, which, while allowing a certain leeway for local variations, often enough formulate broad programs and policies that are binding on their sub-units.[12] Vidich and Bensman provide specific examples of how larger organizations restrict community action in various ways.[13] Small towns and one-industry cities seem to be particularly vulnerable in this respect.

The organizational drift from local to national scope has led to increased decision-making in central headquarters; this is true of both large-scale corporations and unions. Similarly the increase of federal functions and controls in government has progressively narrowed the choices of local officials and leaders. In some cases this development has led more citizens to vote in national

[12] Roland L. Warren, "Toward a Typology of Extra-Community Controls Limiting Local Community Autonomy," *Social Forces* 34:338-341 (May, 1956).

[13] Vidich and Bensman, op. cit., p. 113.

elections than in local community contests,[14] because, perhaps, they realize the greater importance to them of the issues involved. At any rate it is now important to learn what decisions are left to the local community and to whom they are vitally significant. One thing seems certain and should be kept in mind: community decisions are only partly autonomous.

The apparent power vacuum at the top in Schulze's example of the community with absentee-owned corporations may be a consequence of the fact that the local community is no longer in a position to make decisions significantly affecting corporate interests. On the other hand, this situation may represent a power potential rather than a power vacuum. Corporations with local branches may decide not to throw their weight around in smaller communities, but these firms hold in reserve a weapon of great effectiveness, namely, the ability to move any local plant to a different location. In towns where employment is mainly dependent on one or two large companies, a decision to relocate manufacturing units can disrupt the entire economic base of the community. Although such decisions depend on national and international market and supply conditions, they are related to local political factors also. Absentee-owned corporations pay a disproportionate share of taxes in small towns; as a result the local government refrains from changing the tax structure drastically upward for this would kill the goose that lays the golden egg. As long as this tax situation continues, corporations can afford to maintain the kind of hands-off policy noted by

[14] V. O. Key, Jr., *Politics, Parties and Pressure Groups,* 4th ed., p. 627 (New York, Crowell, 1958).

Schulze. But such abdication of power is conditional rather than fixed policy.

Hart, in his study of Windsor, Ontario, presents quite a different power configuration from those sketched above. As he reports it, this community is dominated by four major groups: big business (Ford and Chrysler), the Roman Catholic Church, the unions, and finally the local business group including the Chamber of Commerce. So discrete and cohesive do these groups appear that Hart can find no trace of a general public. Its absence engenders conflicts that are naked and overt. Commenting on the lack of a power pyramid, Hart declares that it may not be clear who "runs the town," but at least "it is not the top management of Ford or Chrysler nor 'stooges' for those managements."[15] McKee, in a similar study, notes the central role of the CIO in Lorain, Ohio, and sees community power in terms of multiple groups combined differently on separate issues. He insists that the familiar pyramidal model seriously distorts many relationships in that city.[16]

Realistic analysis requires more than cross-sectional study of the local community; it must not neglect changes through time. For example, founder-owners of rapidly growing industries have often established family dominance of a corporation, which has gone hand in hand with almost monopolistic power in the local community. Robert and Helen Lynd documented this pattern

[15] C. W. M. Hart, "Industrial Relations Research and Industry," *Canadian Journal of Economics and Political Science* 15:53-73, pp. 59-60, 66, 68 (February, 1949).

[16] James B. McKee, "Status and Power in the Industrial Community: A Comment on Drucker's Thesis," *American Journal of Sociology* 58:364-370, p. 369 (January, 1953).

in their second Middletown volume, showing that the "X family," which founded the local glass jar industry, extended its control into banking, real estate, retail business, education, recreation, religious institutions, charities, the press, and, to a considerable degree, local government.[17] Such dynastic control changes markedly as industry passes from family to managerial dominance. Any power shifts within industry bring in their train other shifts in community power as local familial controls are replaced by specialized management and as labor unions develop; further changes result when local plants are sold outright to absentee-owned corporations.

Consequently any attempt to assess the organization of power in the local community must take into account the stage of maturation of its industry. It is perhaps too early to agree with Daniel Bell that "by and large, the system of family control is finished."[18] For example, one reason that Hunter's Regional City reveals such a marked hierarchical power pattern seems to be that hereditary wealth dominates business activity in that Southern metropolis; at least twenty-five out of Hunter's top forty leaders were so assisted in gaining positions of economic prominence.[19] There may be important regional differences in this respect; Schulze hints that the prevalence of family control in the South seems to be greater than it is elsewhere.[20]

Studies of changing power configurations over time

[17] Robert S. Lynd and Helen M. Lynd, *Middletown in Transition, A Study in Cultural Conflicts,* Chapter 3 (New York, Harcourt, Brace & Co., 1937).

[18] Daniel Bell, "The Power Elite—Reconsidered," *American Journal of Sociology* 64:238-250, p. 248 (November, 1958).

[19] Miller, op. cit., p. 307.

[20] Schulze, op. cit., p. 8.

would also probably show an increasing prominence of formerly submerged groups in American community life. Arnold Rose, commenting on this historic shift in the power balance, says that "now a significant proportion of the lower classes is organized into labor unions and a significant proportion of ethnic minorities have organized into reform groups; and both are participating in political organizations. Thus both the lower classes and the ethnic minorities today have a significant measure of power."[21] This change should be investigated in its relation to industrial maturation in different types of cities.

Generalizations such as Peter Rossi's statement, "the less diversified the economic base of the community, the more clustered is the power,"[22] do not appear to be applicable to all types of American communities. As we have seen, this proposition neglects those cases where absentee-owned corporations abdicate their power or where the rapid growth of unions in other industrial towns broadens the base of power distribution patterns.

While a good many American communities are notably similar in preferring non-governmental to governmental controls, the plurality of power distribution in the wider societal area seems to preclude any uniform pattern. In some cases a commonly shared value system may impose a good deal of uniformity; in other situations the economic organization results in multiple power configurations for which as yet no adequate classi-

[21] Arnold Rose, "Power Distribution in the Community Through Voluntary Association," *Problems in Social Psychology, An Interdisciplinary Inquiry,* J. E. Hulett and Ross Stagner, eds., p. 80 (Urbana, Ill., University of Illinois, 1952).

[22] Peter H. Rossi, "Community Decision-Making," *Administrative Science Quarterly* 1:415-443, p. 440 (March, 1957).

fication has been made. At the present stage of knowledge, social scientists are limited, for the most part, to searching out and reporting the unique power distribution in each community investigated. Yet structural similarities, as well as differences, are revealed in these community studies. This fact suggests that it may soon be possible to work out a typology of communities in terms of economic and social structure, including their functional relationships with the wider society. If this happens it will transcend the traditional distinctions of urban sociology which classifies communities into the broader and less useful categories of institutional cities, trading centers, metropolitan cities, and resort towns.[23] The use of local power patterns will be helpful to sharpen our analysis and furnish a new typology.

The Selection of Issues

What issues are decided at what levels in American communities? George Belknap and Ralph Smuckler found in a Midwest city that the top leadership remains constant, whatever the issue, while lower echelon leaders change in accordance with the problem.[24] Miller, on the other hand, reports considerable fluidity among key influentials as issues change.[25] Research into the reasons for this conflicting evidence should uncover more basic factors affecting community issues. Hunter, for example,

[23] Svend Riemer, *The Modern City,* pp. 41-44 (New York, Prentice-Hall, 1952).

[24] George Belknap and Ralph Smuckler, "Political Power Relations in a Mid-West City," *Public Opinion Quarterly* 20:73-81, p. 81 (Spring, 1956).

[25] Miller, op. cit., pp. 306, 310.

mentions the fact that many issues are bandied about by subleaders; in due time they emerge for top level policy consideration.[26] The initiation of issues and the decisions about them may occur at quite different levels in the power structure.

James Coleman has furnished a trenchant analysis of community issues when they become matters of controversy or conflict. He distinguishes between the initiation of conflict and its perpetuation. In the initiatory phase, three major areas of life provide what Coleman calls bases of response to controversial issues. The first is the economic area, where conflicts arise over items like taxes or the movement of a factory to town; the second is the area of authority, where disputes about such things as city-manager plans and proportional representation arise; the third area consists of cultural values or beliefs, as when disagreements arise over the educational philosophy of school superintendents or about desegregation. Coleman notes that conflicts over cultural values take place especially in cities where there is a rapid influx of inhabitants with different styles of life, in suburban communities, and in Southern towns.[27]

Throughout his discussion, Coleman observes two additional bases of response in the perpetuation stage: attachments or identifications with individuals or groups already involved in the dispute ("psychological") and associational membership that limits word-of-mouth discussions by restricting communication to specific channels ("sociological"). Associational ties seem to have greater influence on middle and upper class persons than

[26] Hunter, op. cit., p. 225.

[27] James S. Coleman, *Community Conflict,* pp. 6-7 (Glencoe, Ill., The Free Press, 1957).

on those of lower status; personal attachments play a greater role in small towns than in larger ones. In both the initiatory and later stages of controversy, the national climate of opinion may be pivotal, as it was during the McCarthy era when labor unions took no stand on the issue because of divided opinion within the membership. Coleman also observes that people who are weakly identified with the community at large (found especially among the lower classes and newer migrants) are apt to overstep the bounds of legitimate methods more quickly when aroused.[28]

Coleman has advanced our general knowledge about the operation of controversial issues in the community; power analysis raises additional questions. What issues are kept out of the arena of public discussion and what problems are allowed to reach the attention of the community? Is there a mechanism for keeping sensitive issues away from the public, and is it used by the private leaders who already possess significant power? This problem is important because the selection of issues—at least public issues—precedes the making of decisions. Often the local newspaper plays a significant role by accenting or exaggerating some problems while minimizing others or eliminating them entirely. Not only does the average citizen perceive the issues as they are revealed in the organs of public opinion, he has a tendency to accept the assigned importance of the issues themselves. Value preferences of the editor or publisher (sometimes related to his clique position) may be a key to the community perception of issues as presented in his newspaper, and these may reflect the views of top-level leaders.

[28] Coleman, op. cit., pp. 13, 21.

Community issues thus furnish an important lead to two significant questions: How do these issues serve as channels for the operation of power structures already firmly set in the community? How do they supply focal situations for change in the community power balance? Hunter and his associates suggest how this problem may be approached when they indicate that a new issue raises three questions in the minds of community leaders: (1) who is behind this thing? (2) how much is it going to cost? (3) what will it do to my business or my agency or my reputation? [29]

Role Images of Leaders

Public opinion, changeable and vacillating as it may be, has a definite bearing on the way in which power is exercised in the community. Community confidence in its leadership, both formal and informal, often determines what can or cannot be done by those who wield one type of authority or another. Assume for a moment that in a given community the role of private leaders has more legitimacy than that of public leaders in the local government. What happens when the public loses confidence in its private top leadership? Probably one of two things will occur: the public will raise its estimation of public authorities and demand that they do something or it will minimize the present mistakes of private leaders and laud them for what they have achieved for the community in the past. The issue will

[29] Floyd Hunter, Ruth Connor Schaffer and Cecil G. Sheps, *Community Organization, Action and Inaction,* p. 33 (Chapel Hill, N.C., University of North Carolina Press, 1956).

die down, and eventually the public will restore its belief in top leadership as a kind of prop for security feelings.

However there is not one public but many. Will people at different levels in the class structure have the same role images of their leaders? David Riesman and Nathan Glazer declare that "only the more disabused folk in the lower strata nourish the myth that there is an inner circle which knows how to manage them and to manage events." [30] Is this statement true or does it reflect certain assumptions about the class structure that are unproved? [31] Riesman and Glazer make their assertion confidently without the use of supporting evidence, so it is only natural for doubts to appear. At any rate, further research is definitely needed to determine how much difference there is in the way people at various socio-economic levels perceive both public and private authorities. This would furnish an invaluable clue to the way in which such leaders could or could not manipulate the masses.

On the other hand, the self-images of leaders have a great deal to do with the way they exercise their authority. Norton Long distinguishes the self-images of governmental and non-governmental leaders in the following way: "The politicians who hold the offices do not regard themselves as governors of the municipal territory but largely as mediators or players in a particular game that makes use of the other inhabitants." Informal

[30] David Riesman and Nathan Glazer, "Criteria for Political Apathy," *Studies in Leadership,* A. W. Gouldner, ed., p. 517 (New York, Harper & Bros., 1950).

[31] Leonard Reissman, *Class in American Society,* pp. 196-202 (Glencoe. Ill., The Free Press, 1959).

leaders, on the other hand, are often "genuinely reluctant, fearful, and even morally shocked at their positions' becoming that of a recognized territorial government."[32] If this applies to all communities, we would have to conclude that even though power is desired, responsibility may not be. It seems likely that there is greater variability from one city to another on this issue than Long suggests. At any rate, a more thorough assessment of the way community power-holders view themselves will furnish a clue to the way they exercise their leadership.

Finally, how do community leaders view the public? Riesman and Glazer speak of upper-level leaders as feeling "mastered by vague events" and of how often they claim that public opinion will not "stand for" this or that policy; frequently such leaders "take refuge behind public opinion for their own inability to act."[33] Here again we may have an insight rather than the statement of a trend. But the issue has crucial significance; what are the images of the public held by dominant community leaders and what are the reciprocal role images of the leaders entertained by their followers? This sort of information can single out important factors in the climate of public opinion that have special relationship to the way different forms of power may be exercised.

In this final chapter we have reviewed enough of the literature on community power studies to give the reader a few salient points of reference which he can apply to his own city or town. It is hoped in this way to furnish not a mere intellectual exercise but a method of analysis

[32] Long, op. cit., pp. 255, 259.
[33] Riesman and Glazer, op. cit., p. 514.

that will help him to see the political process in sociological terms. In summary, some of the questions that may be found useful are: Who are the formal and informal leaders and what is their relationship to each other? What is the shape of the power structure? What is the stage of industrial maturity locally? What is the tradition of past decision? Who are the people most committed and least committed to the community as a focus of loyalty? What are the modes of formal and informal control? What is the role of the political party in joining the two? What types of decision depend chiefly on forces outside the community? How are issues selected for community decision and at what level? How do newspaper policies and the treatment of issues in the press affect the public? How much confidence is invested in both formal and informal leaders? How do members of the community at different socio-economic levels view the community leaders? How do the leaders see their own role and the role of the public?

Questions like these will perhaps reveal more than asking how many Democrats or how many Republicans there are in the city. At any rate, answers to such questions will help the reader to understand the enlargement of perspective, the excitement of exploration, and the satisfaction at reaching even tentative conclusions that motivate the social scientist in his study of power.

VII

Summary and Retrospect

When social values are in transition, people become increasingly preoccupied with the problem of power. It is quite natural that the upheavals of the twentieth century have redirected attention to that problem. Contemporary approaches to power, however, differ appreciably from those of tradition which has taught us so much: Plato, Aristotle, Machiavelli, and Hobbes.

In the first place, there is a widespread awareness of totalitarianism as the most massive concentration of power in history. Endowed with the instruments of advanced science and technology, its leaders assume the direction of industry, agriculture, trade, commerce, finance, military forces, foreign relations, associational life, leisure, the arts, and recreation. Through monopolistic control of propaganda they shape the social myths of an entire people, exercising thought control never before attempted on so large a scale. From the outside, at least, the totalitarian way of life appears almost invincible; and its cardinal position focuses sharp attention on the new power dimensions of our world.

The modern context of the problem differs in another way from that of earlier epochs with the rapid development of scientific methods for investigating power. Since the time of Max Weber, who was one of the first to formulate a more pluralistic and matter-of-fact analysis, social scientists have been developing a more promising approach to this difficult subject. Anthropology, social psychology, and sociology are using new tools of analysis to supplement the orientations of more traditional disciplines. Empirical and objective research brings with it relief from the moralisms, fears, or unabashed glorifications of power that biased so many writings in the past; even the liberal view that power should be hedged with restrictions and dissolved into legal relationships so that we may have a government of laws and not of men shows a strong distrust of power. The contrasting view of the social scientist that power is a natural phenomenon, which gains its constructive or destructive characteristics from the social context is salutary in an era when old valuations are changing and revaluations are going to depend on rational deliberation informed by positive knowledge.

This brief introduction will, I hope, serve as a gateway to serious and scientific study of power as a process with which we must all come to terms, pragmatically and intellectually. The study offers to the reader an analysis of the central features of power, its forms in the simpler societies, its modifications in the more complex civilizations, its contributions to social change, and its manifestations in smaller social units like communities. Perhaps it will allow the reader to establish enough familiarity with the empirical operations of power that he can challenge for himself the myths of its inevitable corrupting force or its inevitable brutalizing tendencies—ideas that have led to withdrawal or escapism and undermine the very foundations of responsible citizenship. The view that power, like electricity or other natural forces, must first be scientifically investigated and understood before it can be properly applied to the service of man is one that holds out sober encouragement in a social climate too easily alarmed by the rapid inroads of totalitarianism. The promise of such a change in the outlook on power has potentialities for human advance if it is fully accepted and put to work.

Selected Readings

Bell, Daniel, "The Power Elite—Reconsidered," *American Journal of Sociology* 64:238-250, November 1958.

A trenchant analysis of C. Wright Mills's *The Power Elite*. Includes significant comments on the configurations of power in America.

Coleman, James S., *Community Conflict* (Glencoe, Ill., The Free Press, 1957).

A concise and illuminating analysis of the ways in which local community conflict originates and continues; important implications for the student of power.

Coser, Lewis A., *The Functions of Social Conflict* (Glencoe, Ill., The Free Press, 1956).

A significant essay on the positive contributions of struggle and conflict to social change; sophisticated in its interpretations of power.

Dahl, Robert A., "Hierarchy, Democracy and Bargaining in Politics and Economics," *Research Frontiers in Politics and Government* (Washington, D.C., The Brookings Institution, 1955).
A significant discussion of three alternative power distributions in the community and their implications for democracy.

Friedrich, Carl J., ed., *Totalitarianism* (Cambridge, Mass., Harvard University Press, 1954).
A series of important essays by specialists on the actual working of totalitarian governments and their use of power.

Gross, Feliks, *The Seizure of Political Power in a Century of Revolutions* (New York, Philosophical Library, 1958).
The most important single-volume analysis of communist strategy and tactics both in the Soviet Union and in the countries dominated by communism since World War II.

Hunter, Floyd, *Community Power Structure, A Study of Decision-Makers* (Chapel Hill, N.C., University of North Carolina Press, 1953).
A pioneering attempt to analyze the organization of power in an American city; important for initiating new research trends for social scientists.

Key, V. O., Jr., *Politics, Parties and Pressure Groups,* 4th ed. (New York, Thomas Y. Crowell Co., 1958).
A lively empirical account of the way in which power becomes shaped and organized in American political processes. Abounding in graphic illustrations and shrewd comment.

Kornhauser, Arthur, ed., *Problems of Power in American Democracy* (Detroit, Wayne State University Press, 1957).
A series of lectures and discussions on power in American society and its relation to democratic values.

Lasswell, Harold D., and Kaplan, Abraham, *Power and Society, A Framework for Political Inquiry* (New Haven, Yale University Press, 1950).
A highly theoretical but provocative attempt to present a unified conception of power. Indispensable for the advanced student.

MacIver, Robert M., *The Web of Government* (New York, Macmillan, 1947).
A penetrating socio-philosophical essay on power and authority in the simpler and more complex forms of government; unmatched in sophisticated interpretation of the many-sided social forces involved. Should not be missed by the serious student.

Mills, C. Wright, *The Power Elite* (New York, Oxford University Press, 1956).
A unique and highly readable marshaling of evidence to show the increasing concentration of

power in a few hands during America's preoccupation with the cold war.

Moore, Barrington, Jr., *Political Power and Social Theory* (Cambridge, Mass., Harvard University Press, 1958).
A brief but stimulating volume on the acquisition and maintenance of power in different societies and historical epochs. Original and penetrating in its judgments.

Neumann, Franz, *The Democratic and the Authoritarian State* (Glencoe, Ill., The Free Press, 1957). (published posthumously)
Important though uneven essays on power configurations in democratic and autocratic regimes, both ancient and modern.

Reissman, Leonard, *Class in American Society* (Glencoe, Ill., The Free Press, 1959).
The only book in American sociological literature that gives thorough attention to the power dimension as related to our stratification system. Suggestive and illuminating.

Russell, Bertrand, *Power, A New Social Analysis* (New York, W. W. Norton, 1938).
A fresh and lively approach to the problems of power by an outstanding philosopher, who writes with wit and charm. Especially valuable for the student approaching the subject for the first time.

Schapera, I., *Government and Politics in Tribal Societies* (London, Watts, 1956).
A comparative study of the development of political

power in African preliterate societies. Useful for clarifying the power structures in "simpler" societies.

Srinivas, M. N., "Dominant Caste in Rampura," *American Anthropologist* 61:1-16, February 1959.
A first-rate analysis of the power dimensions related to caste dominance in an Indian village.

Vidich, Arthur J., and Bensman, Joseph, *Small Town in Mass Society: Class, Power, and Religion in a Rural Community* (Princeton, Princeton University Press, 1958).
A discerning portrayal of the activities and processes of an upstate New York rural community, done in such a way as to reveal its power operations and structures in remarkable detail.

Weber, Max, *The Theory of Social and Economic Organization,* tr. by A. M. Henderson and Talcott Parsons (Glencoe, Ill., The Free Press, 1947).
Sections III and IV provide the fundamental starting point for the modern sociological analysis of power; most valuable for the student thoroughly familiar with European history.

Wittfogel, Karl, *Oriental Despotism, A Comparative Study of Total Power* (New Haven, Yale University Press, 1957).
A somewhat one-sided attempt to analyze various governmental structures in terms of their control of irrigation and thus of masses of men. The volume is nevertheless full of suggestive detail on actual political, economic, and social components of power having great value for the student.